Brassies, Mashies, & Bootleg Scotch

GROWING UP ON AMERICA'S
FIRST HEROIC GOLF COURSE

BILL KILPATRICK

UNIVERSITY OF NEBRASKA PRESS • LINCOLN & LONDON

Library of Congress Cataloging-in-
Publication Data
Kilpatrick, Bill.
Brassies, mashies, and bootleg scotch: growing up on America's first heroic golf course /
Bill Kilpatrick.
   p.   cm.
ISBN 978-0-8032-3642-4 (cloth: alk. paper)
1. Golf courses—United States. 2. Golf
courses—United States—Anecdotes.
3. Kilpatrick, Bill. 4. Fathers and sons. I. Title.
GV981.K55 2011
796.35206873—dc22
2011012749

Set in Iowan Old Style by Bob Reitz.

For Bill and for Rob, and in memory of a girl named Nan

Contents

Brassies, Mashies, and Bootleg Scotch

Introduction

IN ALL THAT HAS BEEN WRITTEN about golf in the six-hundred-plus years of its recorded history, most has been about playing the game, about the great championships, the memorable stars, the great courses and how they came into being, or about the equipment and accessories with which it is played. But other than for those concerned—the trade, as it were—not much has been written about the care and feeding of golf courses and about the usually nameless and faceless men and women who make the game's playing conditions possible.

This is understandable. Unless you're fascinated by equipment with which turf is cultivated and maintained, intrigued by the properties and uses of fertilizers, fungicides, insecticides, pesticides and the like to which golf course turf is subjected, or are a student of water quality and irrigation, or someone to whom footprints in bunkers are an affront, the underside of golf makes for rather heavy lifting.

Millions, in person and through the medium of television, may thrill to a spectacular shot by a charismatic Tiger Woods, say, but the pulse of only a few will quicken to the debut of a new greens mower, a new aerator, a new sprinkler head. As the profusion of gadgetry and specialized appliances and machines has radically altered our day-to-day lives, it also has altered the ways in which golf courses today are maintained. But there was a time when the process was labor-intensive for both man and beast, and it was my good fortune to grow up during the transition from artisanship, experience, and instinct to technology and research-center science. I was privileged to witness personally, overhear, learn of, and take part in a side of golf and a lifestyle that once was and never again will be.

In many respects it was a magic time.

· 1 ·

The Founding Father, Part I

I CALLED HIM DAD, Daddy when I was younger, and more often than not as the years went by I called him Pop. He called me Willie. I referred to him as my father, my dad, and the Old Man. His name was William, known as Bill, and he remains indelible in my consciousness.

He was a greenkeeper, a term he preferred to "golf course superintendent," deeming the latter a bit pretentious. Several of golf's Olympians — Old Tom Morris, being one — had been known primarily as greenkeepers, and thus it was deemed a profession to which there was some cachet. It meant "keeper of the green," the man in charge, management, someone who, depending upon the extent of that for which he was responsible, was likely to hold sway over a crew of laborers. Originally the "green" referred to the village or town green, perhaps a park of some sort; only later did it refer to a golf course.

Although born in Dumfries in western Scotland, my father

did most of his growing up in St. Andrews — the mecca of golf, hard by the North Sea — where his stepfather, a Victorian semi-monster known wryly to my father and his younger sister as "Gentleman Charles," was a master lithographer employed by a firm called W. C. Henderson & Son, at the time (around 1900) one of the largest printing firms in North Britain. Gentleman Charles, apart from his familial heavy-handedness, was a member of a "historic Fife Golf Club" called the St. Andrews Golf Club and in fact won club handicap medals in 1905 and 1908.

As a boy my father loved and played well the game Americans call soccer, but of course he also played golf, as did just about all of his St. Andrews peers and pals, among them 1921 British Open Champion Jock Hutchison. To them the ability to play this most demanding of games was deemed nothing special, not unlike American kids playing baseball. Some were better than others, surely, but playing golf was a thing boys (and a few girls) did as naturally and as routinely as breathing. Accordingly, a prevailing contention in the St. Andrews of the time was that any layabout could play golf whereas a greenkeeper, a figure of management in a golf course operation, mind you, was someone to be looked up to. Unlike today's pecking order in golf, at that time and place being a greenkeeper rather than a mere golf professional was the more desirable, exalted position.

For one thing, a greenkeeper in the Scotland of a hundred years ago only occasionally encountered the golfers who played his course and thus was not obliged, as was routinely done by the resident professional, to tip his cap to those who deemed such mild obsequiousness their due. Walter Hagen, the flashy American superstar who, among other things, is credited with introducing black-and-white golf shoes to 1920s Great Britain, blithely ignored such convention; "The Haig" rubbed elbows with princes. Referring to the lot of British golf professionals before and even after the advent of Hagen, humorist Stephen Potter, in his book *Golfmanship*, wrote truthfully, "We liked our professionals to be quiet and quietly clothed, salt-of-the-earth and with a way of calling you 'sir' which meant that we were all free men but shared a sense of degree, priority and place." That was a mind set of which my father would have none, either for himself or for me and my one and only brother, older by nine years.

Keep in mind that golf in the Scotland of the turn of the twentieth century, unlike its first few decades in the United States, was an Everyman activity, not a game played only by the affluent. Most golf courses were municipal entities played on by any townie with a couple of clubs and the wherewithal to pay the modest green fees then charged. (As late as 1957 I played the famed Old Course in St. Andrews, as always a public course, for "four-and-six," four shillings and sixpence, then equivalent to little more than a dollar.) Keep in mind, too, that the times being what they were—that is, hard—a youngster who could call more than one or two clubs his own, however aged and battered, was envied. Thus most youngsters who played with any degree of frequency were forced to become shot-making virtuosos.

For example, by laying open or hooding its face, by placing it forward or back in his stance, and by gripping up or down on the length of its shaft, my father, even in his declining years, could perform miracles with what he called a mashie (a 5-iron). And the beauty of it was that he considered his ability to do so nothing special; it was just something he could do, and he had difficulty understanding why my brother and I couldn't do it as well as he did. To this day when I trudge warily into a greenside bunker armed with the latest in sand wedge technology, I think back to seeing the Old Man lay open a 5-iron almost on its back and deftly loft his ball onto the green.

We didn't play together very often, my father and I, but on the occasions we did go out for a few after-work holes, when the afternoon shadows were becoming long and the sky was turning to gold, he never carried more than a spoon (a 3-wood), a 5-iron, and a putter, all three held in the crook of his arm as we walked along. In his pocket at such times were a couple of peg tees and a spare ball. He might, if he thought of it, wear his golf shoes. Otherwise, his street shoes served.

His swing was of the old guttie ball era–type, lacking modern aesthetics, perhaps, but all business. Teeing off, his stance wide, he brought the club back in a broad, sweeping motion, then reversed its path to send the ball away — initially on a low trajectory that soon saw it climb sharply before dropping gently to the ground. And he could putt! Oh, man, could he putt! Quickly, too. He'd stand a few feet behind the ball, almost instantly make up his mind as to the proper line, then step up and, with no hesitation and a somewhat wristy stroke, send the ball on its way. If it didn't go in, you could count on it being within a foot or two of the cup.

My brother later told of caddying for the Old Man when the bet was a case of bootleg scotch. This would have been about 1930, when I was about five and my father was the greenkeeper at Sunningdale Country Club in Scarsdale, New York, a suburb of New York City. The opposition was furnished by Sunningdale golf professional Elmer "Whitey" (so called because of his very blond hair and eyebrows) Voight and his assistant, an Irishman named Maurice Walsh. My father's partner was the cigar-chewing caddymaster, a burly, sunny man named Johnny Masley, who at the time was known throughout the greater metropolitan New York area as being very long off the tee. I can't recall being told what the others shot, but my brother reported the Old Man shot 68 and that he and Masley won the case of booze in a breeze.

In the waning days of Prohibition I emulated my father in being a fan of the New York baseball teams, especially the Giants, and one day I came in from playing with a neighborhood kid and found my father and two other men seated at our kitchen table having a postgolf highball. Goggle-eyed, I was introduced to Giants pitcher Hal Schumacher and outfielder Jo-Jo Moore (I *think* it was Jo-Jo Moore). What I remember clearest is Schumacher telling me my daddy was quite a golfer, that he'd shot 71 and had won all the money.

But despite his skills, he rarely played. Golf was his living, the means by which he supported his family, not his recreation. Rather, he was a not very successful student of the running horse, and the off-work days to which he looked forward were spent at Belmont, Aqueduct, Jamaica, at old Empire City in Yonkers, or any track within reasonable driving distance of wherever he happened to be. He was what sportswriter Red Smith referred to as "a producer for the game," which is to say that unlike the professional gambler who goes to a track and bets with both hands on one or maybe two races, the Old Man bet the full card, including the daily double. Every now and then he'd come away a winner, such occasions usually resulting in my mother and I, and later my wife and children as well, being taken out to dinner.

The first president of the PGA (Professional Golfers' Association of America), founded in 1916, was a St. Andrews man named Bob White, among other things honored as the patron saint of Myrtle Beach, South Carolina, golf. He was spoken of almost reverently in our household because through White a number of young Scotsmen of a hundred years ago came to this country to take up positions as professionals or greenkeepers — sometimes both — at golf courses then being built throughout the United States. One of these young men was my father, who arrived in this country in 1908 and went to work immediately for brothers Alec and Jack Pirie,

William Kilpatrick, newly arrived from St. Andrews, drove one of Westchester County's first gasoline-powered fairway mowers at Siwanoy Country Club, then located in what was the Hunt's Woods section of Mount Vernon, New York. Jack Pirie (*center*) was Siwanoy's professional, Alec Pirie (*right*) its greenkeeper. The year was 1908. (Photo courtesy of the author.)

greenkeeper and professional, respectively, at Siwanoy Country Club, then in a section of Mount Vernon, New York, known as Hunt's Woods. From the Pirie brothers and from Bob White my father learned his profession, which a few years later he put on temporary hold for a better-paying job as a chauffeur for, among others, old-time vaudevillians Willie and Eugene Howard.

After serving in France with the U.S. Army Signal Corps' Second Aero Squadron during World War I, he returned to chauffeuring, soon thereafter receiving a call from Bob White to oversee the crew building the course at Century Golf Club in White Plains, New York.

The gang of laborers the Old Man was called upon to supervise at Century were principally Chinese, which presented a problem of communication—quite apart from them not having a clue as to what they were building. My father knew not a word of Chinese other than those to be found on a Chinese restaurant menu, and none of the work gang spoke English. Yet somehow he was able, probably by demonstration and a smattering of pidgin English, to communicate what he wanted done.

My brother used to tell of driving with the Old Man to the Century job site early on Monday mornings to rouse the men out of the bunkhouse in which they lived and slept. Many of them, paid in cash for the week at the end of their half-day's work on Saturdays, would take the train from White Plains into New York, there to spend the night in the city's Chinatown engaged in heaven knows what exotic pursuits—pursuits that seemed to render them difficult to awaken on Monday mornings. Armed with the handle of a pick axe, my father would roar into the bunkhouse and rattle the axe handle on the uprights of the bunk beds in which the men slept, all the while exhorting them at the top of his voice to rise and shine. It was a job phase a St. Andrews lad of the time would be hard-pressed to imagine himself ever performing.

The job at Century completed, Bob White urged my father to take the position of greenkeeper at Sunningdale, a course designed originally by Seth Raynor and later overhauled by famed golf course architect A. A. Tillinghast.

In 1934 the Old Man was lured away from what assuredly would have been a lifetime sinecure at Sunningdale to become the greenkeeper at The Maidstone Club in East Hampton, New York. Maidstone then had two full-length eighteen-hole courses, and I assume the challenge of the larger assignment coupled with the higher salary he was offered prompted his decision to relocate. Nonetheless, he cared very much for Sunningdale and had done an outstanding job in seeing its course progress from wobbly beginnings to mature beauty. In a note handwritten to my father in 1929, Tillinghast referred to the Old Man's "splendid work." While my father was fond of and grateful to many of Sunningdale's members, he felt it was time to move on to a larger stage.

He hadn't been at Maidstone for more than a few years when he was offered the job of greenkeeper at the National Golf Links of America, then and now one of the nation's premier golf courses. Located on the fringes of Southampton, New York, National borders the sandy bluffs of a large body of water known as Great Peconic Bay, which divides the fork of Long Island's eastern end. This essentially seaside location

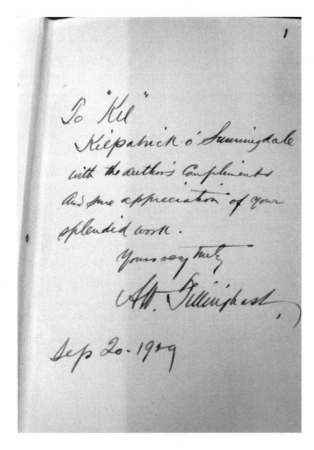

Famed golf course architect A. W. Tillinghast gave my father a copy of his book of golf-related short stories, *The Mutt*, and on one of its endpapers he praised the Old Man's care and feeding of Sunningdale's golf course. (Photo courtesy of the author.)

justifies National's designation as a proper links course. According to revered golf writer Herbert Warren Wind, National was America's "first heroic course." It had been built between 1907 and 1911 to the demanding specifications of a Chicago autocrat named Charles Blair Macdonald, the very first U.S. Amateur Champion and a man of towering and imperious ego.

I don't know how the Old Man and his new boss got along, or even if they ever met, but presumably Macdonald had faith in what my father could do and approved of his hiring. Also, Macdonald was nearing the end of the line, leaving the chain of command to run from the club's board through the chairman of its greens committee, at first a Wall Street lawyer named Morton G. Bogue, later president of the United States Golf Association (1944–45). From all I observed, overheard, and was told, my father and Bogue got along very well; seemingly they liked and trusted each other.

The years at National were the highpoint of the Old Man's career, and for awhile he was one of the metropolitan New York area's best known and most respected golf course superintendents, often called upon to prescribe for the ills of courses within the region. It all ended with the advent of World War II and the decision by National, realizing the course would receive comparatively little wartime play, to reduce the club's overhead; my father's salary, being one of the payroll's highest, was thus deemed most expendable.

He spent a couple of the war years working at Grumman

Aircraft, building fighters for the U.S. Navy. The war over, he contracted to restore to its prewar condition the course at Silver Spring Country Club in Ridgefield, Connecticut. Designed by old mentor Bob White, the course had been allowed to go to seed during the war, and the job of bringing it back proved formidable. I was away as a married G.I. Bill college student at the time and have no firsthand knowledge of what procedures he followed. The job apparently was successfully completed, however, for I recall the restored course as being beautiful.

As the Silver Spring job was nearing its end, my father was asked to have a look at another venerable Long Island course, this one Garden City Golf Club. The home club of its designer, Walter James Travis, another of golf's Olympians and known as the "Grand Old Man," the condition of the course had fallen on hard times, and apparently its board of directors determined my father was the man to return it to its former glory. Expected, however, were instant results, which my father was both unwilling and unable to produce. He wanted the recovery of the course to be slow and permanent, and while he was familiar with various means of "needling" turf growth, he was reluctant to employ them. Impatient with the progress being made on the course, the board gave him the sack. It was a hurtful blow, one from which his pride never really recovered.

He hooked on at nearby Glen Head Country Club (formerly known as Women's National Golf and Country Club) for a couple of unrewarding years, but by then turf-culture science and its accompanying technology had pretty much passed him by. Here again instant results were expected, and the Old Man was incapable of producing them.

When he died at age seventy-four in 1963, he was the road inspector for the Town of Branford, Connecticut.

· 2 ·

Good-bye, Charlie

THE FIRST HORSE OF WHICH I was aware was named Charlie. I couldn't have been more than five or six, and all I knew about him was that he was big and brown and lived in a big green barn where my father had his office.

I had no direct contact with Charlie; I was never boosted up on his broad back, never held the rope attached to his halter, never fed him or watered him, and never cleaned his stall. The latter were jobs done by men who worked for my father. In season, anyway. During the winter months, when the men were laid off, the aging, gray-whiskered Charlie was attended to by either my father or my brother.

At the time—this again was about 1930—my father was at Sunningdale and Charlie was one of the work crew, his principal job being to pull the sickle bar with which the golf course roughs were mowed. Occasionally he'd be called upon to pull a sledge called a stoneboat or maybe a dump rake, but that was about it. In the world of workhorses I suppose it could be said old Charlie had it fairly easy. He was one of what originally had been a team. I don't remember his mate and have no idea what happened to him. But apart from being replaced by a tractor, what happened to Charlie is all too vivid in my memory.

Every now and then during the spring, summer, and fall months, when the golf course was open, I'd be out playing in the yard and I'd hear the unmistakable clackety-clack of the sickle bar as it mowed down the fragrant timothy grass bordering the fairway of nearby No. 4. I'd run over to the chain-link fence that ran along three sides of the yard and watch this mysterious and exotic creature as he plodded along through the deep grass, alternately stopping, starting, and turning in response to the commands of the man riding the sickle bar and holding the reins.

But it was during the off-season months, when the golf course was closed, that I became much more aware of Charlie. It was then that I'd accompany my father or my brother to the barn while one or the other attended to the old horse's needs. Sunningdale had built my family a new house down an embankment some forty or so yards off the fourth tee, and it was only a couple of hundred yards, if that, from the house to the barn area. It was nothing for me to tag along when it was time to feed and water Charlie.

There are three distinct memories here.

The first is of my father, the butt of an unlit cigar clamped firmly in a corner of his mouth, coughing and gently talking to the horse as he shoveled out Charlie's stall, by no means the Old Man's favorite chore. "Move over, you old bugger," he'd say as he shouldered the horse from one side of the stall to the other. Then he was likely to cough as the ammonia fumes from Charlie's copious urine got to him. "Damn, but you're a pisser!" he'd mutter, reaching into a hip pocket for a handkerchief to wipe his watering eyes.

The second memory is of my brother walking Charlie down to a nearby spring and standing by as the horse would take in what to me seemed enough water to fill a bathtub. Water from the spring, located down the hill from the house, filled a yard-square cement-and-rock cistern built a couple of feet above ground; as Charlie neared it my brother would drop the halter rope, and the old horse would jog a few steps up to it and lower his big head to drink.

This well-grooved routine became anything but when the temperature dropped to below freezing; then the water at the top of the cistern would ice over, at times to a depth of three or more inches. Under such circumstances the watering of Charlie required taking along a hatchet with which to break through the ice. As was his custom the old horse would want to jog the last few yards up to the cistern, and my teenage brother's best efforts to hold him back would prove futile. Then ensued a grim (but in reflection, comic) struggle: with one hand my brother would keep shoving Charlie's eager muzzle to one side, while with the other he would swing the hatchet to break the ice so the horse could get at the water. It was high drama, my fear always being that Charlie would be hit in the mouth with the hatchet.

Charlie loved snow. Perhaps he just liked being outdoors after long periods of confinement to his stall, but when taken out on a day on which there was new snow on the ground, he'd jerk the halter rope out of my brother's hand and, snorting and tossing his head, make what passed for a stretch run to the spring, pausing occasionally to kick up his heels, even to drop down and roll in the fresh snow. It was then that he scared me to death; so large a creature free of any restraint could be terrifying to a small boy. What really was scary on such occasions was that he might simply take off, and how would my brother go about telling the Old Man that he'd lost the horse?

The third memory is of Charlie's end.

Although I had no idea what it meant, one morning I overheard my father tell my mother that Charlie was going to be "put down." Anything to do with Charlie interested me, so even if I didn't know what being "put down" meant, I asked if I could watch. Not only was my request firmly denied, but I was told to stay away from the barn area and that I wasn't to leave the yard. Of course at the first opportunity I hied myself to some woods from which I could see the nearby barn and its accompanying sheds. I didn't have long to wait before a state trooper's car pulled up and a uniformed officer got out. My father came out of his office to greet the trooper, and as they were shaking hands I noticed one of the men leading Charlie out of the big barn and around behind a long, low shed in which bags of fertilizer were stored. I scooted through the thicket of trees and scrub to see where the horse was being taken.

Behind the shed I noted a deep and open pit, its freshly dug dirt piled up to one side. The old horse was led to the edge of the pit, where he stood quietly while his halter was removed. Around the corner of the shed came my father and the uniformed trooper. The Old Man walked up to the horse, patted him on the snout a couple of times, said something I couldn't hear, then stepped back as the trooper drew his revolver and fired a bullet into Charlie's graying head.

As planned, I suppose, the old horse fell into the pit on his side and back. My father, the trooper, and the man who had led Charlie out looked down to make certain the horse was dead, and just to make sure the trooper fired two more shots into what I suppose was Charlie's head. Then they walked away, and a couple of the Old Man's men showed up and began shoveling dirt into the pit.

It was about two days before I could look my father in the eye, and to this day whenever I see a draft horse, I picture old Charlie joyously rolling in the freedom of new-fallen snow.

• **3** •

Weed No More

ONE OF THE FIRST aspects of golf of which I became aware was that it involved caddies—boys and young men who in my childish eyes appeared to be semi-deities. Although I had no idea of what was involved in caddying beyond carrying a bag of clubs, it took no effort at all to imagine myself one of them.

Off to the left of the driveway of the house at Sunningdale were steps leading up to a gate in the chain-link fence that bordered three sides of the yard. Once through the gate there was a dirt path running from behind the fourth tee directly to the maintenance barns. To the left of the path was a vegetable garden tended on his off-hours by one of my father's men, a man named Augie Zangara, who was a curiosity to me in that he was missing a couple of fingers. I was told they had been blown away by the mishandling of firecrackers.

Virtually since birth I had been conditioned to be silent and still whenever a golfer was about to hit a shot or stroke a putt, but that didn't prevent me from scrambling up the few steps to the fence gate whenever I saw or heard golfers approaching the tee. Some of them knew who I was and might say, "Hello, Billy. How are you today?" My shy and downcast mumbled reply at such times would be, as I was instructed, "Fine, sir, thank you." That mild discomfort out of the way, I'd peer at the caddies, envious of their uniform caps and jackets and impressed by the seeming nonchalance with which they went about handing their employer a club or a towel.

At that time the term "tee box" was still applied to a wooden box in which could be found wet sand, little hand-formed spires of which were preferred by some golfers to tee up the ball. The making and placing of the spires was often the province of the caddies, and I used to admire the speed and dexterity with which they did the job. And I admired and was envious of the casualness with which they slung the strap of their employer's golf bag over their shoulder and headed off down the path leading to the fourth fairway. Absolutely awesome were the older and bigger caddies carrying doubles, and I used to wonder if the day would come when I'd be strong enough to carry two bags of golf clubs. Although none ever did, any one of those days would have been complete had one of the caddies turned to me and said, "Hiya, Billy." My brother caddied every now and then, and because I adored him and wanted to be like him, I couldn't wait until I was old enough to join the caddy ranks.

Most of the caddies were teenagers and young men from

nearby Yonkers, some from Hastings and Dobbs Ferry. Each day during the mid-March to late-October season they were driven to and from Sunningdale in a side-curtained, wooden-benched truck designated "the caddy bus." The caddymaster and driver of the bus was the aforementioned Johnny Masley, invariably seen wearing a white "Ben Hogan–type" golf cap and with the butt of a cigar always present in a corner of his mouth. Although a genial man he was every inch and every ounce master of the caddies. I think he himself lived in Yonkers and knew the names of his charges and where they lived. Each caddy understood that the caddy bus stopped at such-and-such a corner at a certain time each morning, and if a kid wanted or needed a day's work he'd better be there to meet it. Masley tolerated no slackers.

I have no idea how caddies these days learn the do's and don't's of caddying, but back then at Sunningdale, after signifying a desire to caddy, a recruit had to undergo a training regimen prescribed by the caddymaster. For an hour or so, for which an applicant would not be compensated, Masley would describe and demonstrate the basics: the best and proper way to carry a golf bag, the proper organization of the clubs carried therein, where to walk (always ahead of your employer), when to take the bag off your shoulder and present the clubs for a selection by your man, where to stand and when, how to tend the pin, the replacing of divots, the penalties if you were caught stealing anything (especially golf balls) from a player's bag, proper behavior in the fenced caddy yard, when to eat your lunch if you had one, and so on. You'd then be put to the test; you'd caddy for him and perhaps for one of the professionals when a few late-afternoon holes were played. If you passed you'd be paid. If not, back you went to again be instructed in the basics. If caddying just wasn't your thing, Masley was quick to advise another line of work.

For an at-loose teenager or a young man trying to scrape together a few bucks to buy, say, an old Model T Ford, becoming a caddy was a desirable thing. Pretty much throughout the 1930s, the nation — the entire world — experienced a crippling economic depression. In this country alone hundreds of thousands of one-time breadwinners were out of work. Mortgages were foreclosed, savings were exhausted, rice and beans and potatoes and day-old bread became diet staples, clothes were patched and repatched, socks were darned and redarned. With the exception of the well-to-do, most families simply had to get by, and for just about the entire caddy corps of the time any money made carrying some wealthy man's or woman's golf bag contributed to a family's rent and groceries.

There were no guarantees a caddy's services would be required; often a kid would show up and not "get out" to "make a loop" because enough golfers hadn't shown up to assure his hiring. As might be imagined, disappointment often marked a caddy's day; he had to return home empty-handed. I don't know if what I'm about to describe was a Sunningdale original (I doubt it was), but Masley and my father combined to make certain the unemployed caddies hadn't shown up in vain.

The greens at Sunningdale were planted in one of the varieties of grass known as bent, most likely velvet bent. Although thick in texture, a rich, deep green in color, and a superb putting surface if properly mowed and cared for, it was as delicate as a ballerina *en pointe*, and if evening dinner-table talk at our house was any indication it seemed to require constant attendance. Quite apart from the fungal diseases to which the greens were subject, the water and feedings they received in the on-going effort to keep them healthy also encouraged the sprouting in their midst of weeds and occasionally such undesirables as crabgrass.

At the time the use of weed-fighting chemicals wasn't as widespread as it is today—if indeed such remedies were available—meaning most weeds had to be removed by hand. Accordingly, my father, his foreman, and the work crew regularly carried penknives with which any weed spotted on a green or on a tee was cut at its roots and removed. There were times, however, when the entire work crew might be involved in a given project (rebuilding a tee, for example, or clearing brush) or it would rain for a couple of days, meaning on-the-spot weeding of the greens would be on hold. At such times weeds seemed to pop up overnight, and the regular early morning inspection and mowing of the greens would reveal areas that demanded attention.

Since the work crew's time could be more effectively spent on other projects, the decision was made to enlist the underemployed caddies in an on-going program of weed removal.

The kids who didn't get out, usually the younger, less experienced ones, were handed a bucket and an inexpensive penknife and were driven in a truck to certain greens and charged with removal of any and all weeds. The purpose was twofold—the weeds would be extracted, and the kid could go home with at least a few coins in his pocket. I don't know what or how they were paid, but I think it was by the bucketful; if a kid went home with fifty cents, he'd cut out a lot of weeds and the day could be considered reasonably profitable. This hands-and-knees labor by the caddies was loosely supervised by the Old Man, by his foreman (a droll man named Frank Cicciollo), and every now and then by the caddymaster himself.

You should know that my father was one of those fortunate few who can by some wizardry involving thumb and forefinger press both to the lips and emit a shrill, piercing whistle that can be heard at truly incredible distances. Were you to hear it you'd know it was a summons or a warning, a signal to pay attention. I dreaded it throughout my childhood because it meant to come running to face whatever music he had in mind, in my case occasionally punitive in nature. He would use the whistle to scare off deer and other wildlife that had the temerity to trespass on the golf course. Should one or two neighbors of the course sneak on to play a few unauthorized late-afternoon holes, the whistle and a dismissing wave of his right arm would send them packing. The whistle was a formidable weapon, and when my father used it you knew he wasn't kidding.

Early one afternoon, when the weed-removal program had enjoyed a run of perhaps two or three weeks, the Old Man was driving back to his office on one of the golf course roads when he happened upon some caddies down on their knees on the third green. The kids were grouped in a sort of circle and were laughing and pounding each other on the back. They weren't aware of the approach of doom. The piercing blast was sounded, and the startled kids turned and got to their feet. They had been playing mumblety-peg for pennies, the game having replaced any thought of weeding. They were ordered back to the caddy yard on the double and assured their services as removers of weeds on Sunningdale's greens were no longer required.

That was the end of the program. I never did learn what happened to the buckets and knives with which the kids had been equipped, but I like the thought that perhaps among the effects of a man who as a kid in the early 1930s had cut weeds at Sunningdale his heirs found a cheap penknife.

• 4 •

Mixing It Up

I CAN'T LET THE BUSINESS about the penknives go without writing about Harold J. English, his name being among those heard frequently in our house when I was growing up.

To this day I have in the pencil tray in the middle drawer of my desk a cheap penknife, its larger blade open (when I'm dawdling, trying to think of what keys to strike next, I sometimes use the tip of the blade to scrape my fingernails), its "pearl" inserts yellowed with age. In capital letters one of the inserts bears the legend:

HAROLD J. ENGLISH

DOBBS FERRY, N.Y.

TEL. D.F. 3-0325

Whether Harold J. English lived in Dobbs Ferry or just had his business there I can't recall, but I suspect he worked out of his home. I remember him as being a sales representative for a manufacturer of fertilizer, for a supplier of seed, and I think for the long-gone C. B. Dolge Company of Westport, Connecticut, a manufacturer of insecticides. He often called on my father, and over the years they became good friends, although it would be hard to imagine two more dissimilar men. My father's idea of riotous dress, for example, was a paisley-print necktie, whereas Harold J. English was a peacock right out of a 1920s John Held "hotcha" drawing.

Lacking only a thin moustache and sideburns, he looked not unlike a Central Casting gigolo, or perhaps a Prohibition-era hard guy: thinning black hair slicked back and glistening with brilliantine, "five o'clock shadow" at ten o'clock in the morning, pin-striped dark suits, red and white peppermint-striped shirts with French cuffs and cufflinks the size of quarters, florid ties fastened in place with a pearl stickpin, buttoned-up vests, a pinky ring that may have held a real diamond, a stubby black cigarette holder, and, weather warranting, a snugly fitted black Chesterfield overcoat, a white or foulard silk scarf, and, yes, dove-gray spats. Cold weather or no, usually topping off this princely raiment was a black derby worn at a properly rakish angle. What's more he had a toothy smile that revealed good, albeit tobacco-stained teeth, one of which I recall as being gold. Had you seen Harold J. English approaching, your instinctive reaction would have been to hold onto your wallet.

Yet by all accounts he was the nicest, most polite of men, liked very much by both my parents and always welcome in our home, whether on business or socially. For some reason, of all the business Christmas cards that came to the house every year, his was thought of as being personal. And unlike the gift bottles of scotch or boxes of cigars schmoozing salesmen gave my father at Christmas, Harold J. English's gift scotch was thought of as being from one friend to another. There were times, too, when he'd come calling socially, often accompanied by one of his ladyfriends, none of whom I remember.

Why all this sticks in my mind I have no idea. Perhaps it's because of the man's principal stock-in-trade—fertilizer. And I think that may be because of a family euphemism for it, a euphemism that skirted close to a forbidden, and thus tantalizingly appealing, word.

At Sunningdale in those days there was a long, low shed in which sacks of fertilizer were piled on wooden pallets from its dirt floor almost to the roof. The shed was painted dark green and was walled—that is, boarded—along the back and on the ends (it was the shed behind which old Charlie had been dispatched). Across a sort of courtyard, its open front faced the big green barn in which the late Charlie had been stalled and in which my father had his office. In addition to the sacks of fertilizer, the shed housed a big pile of sand and an equally big pile of topsoil. At one end of the shed there was a smaller pile of what was known then (and I guess still is) as topdressing.

On days when it rained steadily and the men were prevented from working on the course, they often were put to the task of mixing topdressing. It was easy, congenial work involving feeding alternate shovelfuls of topsoil, sand, and, every so often, fertilizer into a roaring continuous-belt machine that spewed the resultant mixture out in a conical pile. I don't know what the machine was called, but I understood it to be an essential piece of equipment. Powered by a loud and smoky gasoline engine, its sloped belt consisted of crosswise rows of steel teeth that carried the shoveled-in topsoil, sand, and fertilizer upward at about a forty-degree angle for eight or so feet, forcing it through a sort of steel comb — a perpendicular row of long, rigid teeth.

There was, however, a preliminary step to all this. Near the pile of topsoil and propped up by bolted-on 2x4s at almost forty-five-degree angles were two screens measuring three to four feet wide and perhaps six or seven feet long. Each consisted of an open box frame fashioned of 2x6s. Fastened on one side with bent heavy-duty nails and stretching over the frame's entire width and length was quarter-inch or so wire mesh. At each frame two men alternated in tossing shovelfuls of topsoil to the top of the screen while a third man, the teeth of a garden rake inverted, pushed and pulled the dirt back and forth as it tumbled down the length of the frame, screening out clumps of turf, roots, sticks, and stones that yet a fourth man shoveled up and tossed into a separate pile.

The topsoil thus screened was a joy to a small boy. It felt cool and delightful and could be plunged into with both hands without fear of a cut, breaking a fingernail, or nicking a knuckle. Running through my fingers, it smelled wonderful. Later, when older, I'd read something lyrical about the smell of good, rich, damp earth and know exactly what the writer had in mind. But, invariably, whenever I went to play in it I was shooed away. I never understood why; it was one of those imponderables with which adults torture children eager to find out what's on the other side of the mountain.

Anyway, it was shovelfuls of this screened topsoil that were blended with the sand and fertilizer and spewed by the roaring machine into yet another pile. As the mixture flew out from the conveyor belt, two or three men would rake it back and forth to assure an evenness of blend, the idea being to avoid the possibility of concentrations of fertilizer "burning" the delicate grass on the greens. A blended pile was then hand-shoveled over a couple of times and tossed into still one more pile, there to sit until it was hand-shoveled aboard a small dump truck to be hauled wherever it was needed.

To me at the time the intriguing element in all this was the fertilizer, known euphemistically in our house as "chicken*ship*." It wasn't chicken droppings, of course, which would have generated far too much heat for anything other than the cold frames in which, during winter months, my mother grew fresh herbs. Even so, the more blunt term was applied generically to all fertilizers, and I often overheard the men use it among themselves. I knew what the word meant and couldn't understand why my parents persisted in referring to it as "chicken*ship*." I mean, I could picture a chicken and I could picture a ship, but the best I could do with "chicken*ship*" was a shipload of chickens. Was Harold J. English a dealer in chickens sold by the shipload? And were they then ground up and dried, their remains placed in big paper bags and piled in a Sunningdale shed? I went along with the gag, even referred to it as "chicken*ship*" myself (much to the amusement of my father, I might add), but it was years before I came to appreciate the consideration of my parents for my young and innocent ears.

I never knew what became of Harold J. English. When the Old Man took the job at Maidstone, in those days considered away to hell and gone out on the end of Long Island, he was called on by a different crew of salesmen. The Christmas cards continued for a few years, but I think they represented the last links to the man from Dobbs Ferry.

5

A Badge of Honor

I'VE NEVER BEEN MUCH INTERESTED in celebrities. I've always been interested in people, but celebrity itself never captured my imagination. For one thing I've been in the employ of celebrities, and with few exceptions — very few — I found them consumed by their own celebrity and thus rather hard to take. Still, I very much want to meet and talk with Jon Voight, the actor.

When I was little his father, Whitey Voight, was Sunningdale's head golf professional and a man who when I was with my father always greeted me with a smile and called me by name. As required, kids in those days tended to be "seen and not heard," and when an adult, especially a man whose attention was desired, went out of his way to smile at you and call you by name, you felt special. The visiting ladies in my mother's bridge club cooing over me meant nothing compared to the attention of a man or an older kid, particularly one of the caddies or one of my brother's friends.

Somewhere along the line in the late 1920s or early 1930s the decision was made to have Sunningdale's caddies wear matching caps and jackets. It wasn't exactly unique for caddies to wear uniforms, although not many clubs required them. I may well be living under a rock, but I know of no club now that does, a possible exception being Augusta National (which I always thought of as somewhat chintzy in that the uniform it provided during the Masters appeared on TV to be nothing more than a pair of ordinary work coveralls).

There was nothing chintzy about the jackets and caps worn by Sunningdale's caddies. The material of the jacket was not unlike a soft canvas, the color a sort of burnt orange. The knitted cuffs and the collar were black. A large black "S" was sewn on the breast — I think on the left side. The crown of the baseball-type cap was the same burnt orange in color, the bill black. Front and center on each cap was another black "S," in the same font but smaller than the letter on the jacket.

Apart from the jacket and the cap, what caught my young eye was the numbered badge each caddy was assigned and required to wear on his jacket on the side opposite the letter. It may have been oblong in shape, even round, but I see it in my mind's eye as a five-pointed star. Whatever its shape, what I'm sure of is that I wanted one.

My brother, then in high school, often caddied at Sunningdale and had one of the uniform jackets and a matching cap. He had a numbered badge, too, and occasionally, providing I was persistent in begging to do so, I was allowed to pin it to my sweater and wear it around the house, even while playing outside in the yard. I was under penalty of death if I lost it, which only increased my desire to have one of my very own.

I made no secret of this. At what must have been every opportunity I made my wishes known to my parents and, whenever I saw them, to professional Whitey Voight and caddymaster Johnny Masley. I'm sure my one-note insistence amused those to whom I voiced it, at first, but I'm also sure there were times I was told to knock it off.

At the time, I was too young to be interested in cars. I knew they could be dangerous because a door on the family Chrysler sedan had been slammed on my fingers. My father was the inadvertent slammer, and I remember him crying almost as much as I was when he carried me in his arms into the house, where my wounds were treated and the determination made to take me immediately to our family doctor in the nearby village of Ardsley. Young bones are pliable, and it turned out none were broken, but for months afterward I sat in the car with my hands in my lap.

I can't recall what my father drove by way of a work vehicle (it may have been a Model A Ford sedan), but a few weeks after my crushing experience with the car door whatever he drove pulled into the yard and I was told to get in, that he wanted me to see something. He did this sort of thing from time to time, showing me a tortoise, or a hawk's nest, or some other curiosity in which he knew I'd be interested. I climbed aboard eagerly, wondering what it was I was about to see.

I was clueless, even when we drove to the clubhouse and parked near the path leading up to the golf shop. I got out and fell into step beside him as we walked up the path. Again Whitey Voight greeted me by name when we walked into his shop. Then he said he had something for me. And what he had for me was a my-size Sunningdale burnt-orange caddie jacket, an appropriately small matching caddie cap, and above all a numbered caddy badge. I was ecstatic, and I'm sure that night I put up a spirited argument when my mother insisted I remove both jacket and cap before having my bath and going to bed.

I don't know what happened to the jacket or the cap; I outgrew them, and because I wore both constantly they may well have wound up exhausted and out-at-the-elbows in a bag for the rag man. (In those Depression-mired days, there were itinerant men driving horse-drawn wagons that regularly cruised neighborhoods or coursed country roads seeking old rags. The cry "Old rags! Any old rags?" could be heard throughout an entire block.) And I don't know what became of the badge. Like many things once important to small boys, it, along with supposed arrowheads, "clearie" marbles, and a scrap or two of leather, probably worked its way to the bottom of a cigar box or a shoe box and then one unceremonious day went out with the trash. I'm sorry, too, because I would love to be able to show all of it to Jon Voight when I tell him about his father's thoughtful kindness to a little kid. Years later as an adult I was talking with my father about Sunningdale days, and I mentioned the jacket, cap, and badge and suggested he had arranged them as a gesture of contrition for having slammed the Chrysler door on my fingers. But he said the idea was all Whitey Voight's, that the Chrysler door had nothing to do with it.

Still more years later when I was living in Manhattan, I was shocked and saddened to read in one of the New York dailies that Elmer Voight, golf professional at Sunningdale Country Club in Scarsdale, New York, had been killed in an automobile accident on Central Avenue in neighboring Hartsdale.

He was a nice man.

6

The Grass *Was* Greener

THE OLD MAN TOOK THE JOB at Maidstone in East Hampton, New York, in 1934. In those days Maidstone had two standard-length eighteen-hole golf courses, both laid out on sloping land behind and even among sand dunes fronting the Atlantic Ocean. This proximity to the sea could be a blessing on a hot summer day when breezes blowing in off the ocean provided some relief from the heat. But occasionally the salt air, especially if it was foggy, burned the sensitive grass on the greens; it often contained the spores of attacking fungal diseases such as "dollar spot," a term heard around our house almost as often as "No, you may not."

Dollar spot was what its name implies — roundish, silver dollar–sized spots of grass turned a straw-colored tan by the disease. This is not to be confused with "brown patch," another demon with which the Old Man dueled. I don't know that any of these airborne diseases were fatal to the grass they attacked, but their presence was unsightly to a greenkeeper who during his at least once-a-day rounds regularly stopped to pick up pieces of paper being wafted along on *his* golf courses. "Unsightly" upgraded readily to "ugly," and an ugly golf course was something the Old Man couldn't abide.

Because I have no reason to believe otherwise, his work on the golf courses at Maidstone was exemplary, so much so he was called upon to administer to the club's grass tennis courts, which I recall numbered at least eight. Maintaining grass tennis courts is a much different exercise than maintaining golf course greens. For one thing, unlike putting greens, the former must be dead level over their entire surface. For another, grass tennis courts, if they're to be kept in proper playing condition, must be rolled on a regular schedule; all balls take funny bounces, but a tennis ball that flies off line because of some irregularity on a court's surface is intolerable. On the other hand, regular rolling tends to compact the soil in which the grass is grown, so the weight of the roller is of prime importance—it must be heavy enough to insure an even, level surface, yet not so heavy as to unduly compact the soil.

As indicated earlier my father was a firm believer in sand as well as a process called aeration—punching holes one to two inches deep in the surface of a green (or in this instance, a grass tennis court) and then covering it with topdressing, which in turn, with brooms made of birch twigs, was swept in in a manner right out of a painting by Corot.

Keep in mind, too, that the grass courts were subject to the same diseases as were the putting greens, meaning periodic attacks of this or that fungus or blight. In addition, as with the greens, there were both surface and subsurface insects with which to cope, even the occasional mole. The grass courts presented an added challenge in that they were subject to heavy wear along the baselines, especially at the points at which serves were launched. One reason for building multiple courts, then, was that surface recovery time could be spread out.

The pressure to have as many courts as possible in perfect or almost perfect condition reached its peak each summer when a tournament billed as the Maidstone Invitational was played.

Today's big-time tennis stars are out-and-out professionals, but in the 1930s and earlier the top players in the world were said to be amateurs. I say "were said to be" because everyone knew the game's ticket-selling names were making their living playing tennis. How they were paid I don't know—probably by more than generous expense and travel allowances, perhaps by appearance money, and certainly by under-the-table sleight of hand. Whatever method was used, each season saw several of them playing at Maidstone. You could see such men stars as Don Budge, Gene Mako, Baron Gottfried von Cramm, and Sidney B. Wood, and women stars such as Alice Marble, Sarah Palfrey Cook, and Helen Jacobs.

The tennis professional at Maidstone was a compact and

nimble Scotsman named Ernie Clark, who during the off-season served in a like capacity at New York City's venerable and prestigious Racquet and Tennis Club. He had a son, also named Ernie, who was my age and my summertime knock-around pal. Thanks to that connection and through my father, for one or two summers both Ernie and I were employed during the tournament as ball boys (I can't recall any girls serving in the same capacity). If you've ever watched a big-time tennis match on television, ball boys (and now, in this age of enlightenment, ball girls as well) are those youthful streakers you see darting to and fro in pursuit of stray tennis balls, which then are supplied as needed to the player who is serving.

Ernie's father brooked no nonsense, and after patient but firm drilling as to our duties we were told to show up dressed all in white, including socks and tennis sneakers (although we could wear a brown or black leather belt). I don't recall either Ernie or me or the other ball boys ever wearing any sort of head cover. Above all we were to keep absolutely quiet and remain as inconspicuous as possible, and we had to have the agility and off-the-dime speed of a springbok. I don't remember what we were paid, but I'm certain it was no major contribution to future college tuition or the assembling of a stock portfolio.

It was for me a brief but memorable career. I chased balls for Budge and for Mako, the former's doubles partner, and for Sidney Wood, as well as for Von Cramm and for a pair of pre–World War II wizards from Japan, their names forgotten by me. I also chased balls for Alice Marble and Sarah Palfrey Cook. I worked only the preliminary matches, the final matches being the province of ball boys more experienced and more senior in service. Although I'm sure they did, even if only to say, "Balls, please," I can't recall any one of the stars ever speaking to me.

Throughout all this tournament frenzy my father was the proverbial one-armed paperhanger, dividing long hours each day between overseeing preparation and maintenance of the tennis courts and the daily routines involved in maintaining the golf courses. Somewhere along the line, although not at the same time, he was handed yet another challenge, this one a moonlighting job.

One of the impressive summer houses lining both sides of the road leading to Maidstone's clubhouse was owned by a man named Henry R. Sutphen, the head man of the Electric Boat Company (builder of John F. Kennedy's famed World War II *PT-109*). Sutphen may have been a member of Maidstone and thus would have known who my father was and of his reputation (one admirer later told me this included the ability to "grow grass on a billiard table"). Sutphen wanted the Old Man to build a bowling green in his backyard. This was a job right up my father's alley, for as a youngster in St. Andrews he had lived on Bowling Green Terrace and thus knew exactly what was required.

Building, seeding, and mowing the bowling green took the better part of a summer, and once it was completed my mother and I were taken to see it. To this day it remains in my mind's eye as the greenest grass I've ever seen, and I wonder whatever happened to it or if it even still exists.

A now-and-then golfer at Maidstone in those days—a good golfer, too—was Howard Hughes, and it was said of him at the time that he once turned up for a clubhouse party wearing a tuxedo and tennis sneakers.

7

Boy Explorer

THE SWITCH IN JOBS to the National Golf Links of America in neighboring Southampton was made in the spring of 1938. My brother was away at the Navy school in Annapolis when, on a blustery March day, my mother, my father, and I moved into the greenkeeper's cottage at National, a four-bedroom, one-bath single-story stuccoed structure situated on about two or three acres of land upon which also were a small barn, a small guest house and garage, and a separate two-car garage. The grounds, which included a number of trees as well as a rather large vegetable garden, were within fifty or so yards of National's thirteenth green; a few trees, heavy brush, and undergrowth separated and masked it from the back of the guest house and the garage. Access to the property, which bordered a public road, was gained through iron gates mounted on two massive pillars, each topped by a large round concrete ball (a youthful challenge was to climb one of the pillars and

The greenkeeper's cottage at National. Toward the end of a
working day I'd sit on the curb and wait for my father's
pickup to come down the road from the barns.
(Photo courtesy of the author.)

embrace its ball). Once through the gates, the cottage and its
driveway were off to the immediate right.

If you continued on the paved private road for perhaps a
quarter-mile or so, you'd come to the maintenance barns and
to a large shed in which bags of fertilizer were piled and topdressing was mixed. Atop a sloping bank behind the U-shaped
main barn area was the elevated tee for No. 6, a 131-yard par-3,
its undulating green within about thirty yards of a section of

the barn that housed two massive (to my young eyes) electrically powered Worthington pumps that made possible irrigation of the entire golf course.

Just along the paved road from the cottage, a distance of perhaps a hundred yards, were three ponds. Originally there had been a fairly wide tidal inlet off a large but shallow body of water called Bull's Head Bay that in turn emptied into and was fed by Great Peconic Bay. The first of the ponds was formed when the public road leading to Great Peconic Bay's shoreline (and to National's clubhouse, yacht basin, and bathhouse) was built, the second when the road leading to the maintenance barns was built, the third with the building of an earthenware walkway from the thirteenth tee to the road and the thirteenth green, the latter two probably when the course was being built.

Underneath the road leading to the barns was a culvert through which there was always a flow of water. I can't recall a culvert being under the walkway, but perhaps there was one. In any event, over the years the water on one side of the walkway—fed by springs, perhaps, and certainly by rain runoff—had become progressively less saline, so much so it supported a gratifying population of freshwater perch. The smaller pond in front of the thirteenth tee was brackish and in my experience comparatively fishless. The pond between the barn road and the public road was saltier and rich in eels and blue crabs. The water in the large shallow bay was saltwater, period, its bottom here and there a source of flounders caught using kernels of canned giblet corn as bait. There was a large culvert under the public road, and on certain nights the water coursing through it was rich in glowing, flashing phosphorous.

There was scrubland across the barn road opposite the cottage and thick woods on the other side of the public road. Deer and rabbits were common sights, and a pair of swans frequented the ponds on either side of the earthenware walkway, the male testy and dangerous when he and his mate were harboring a signet. If he charged you, his big wings extended, he could break a bone, which he did to one of my father's crew, the man suffering a cracked fibula. Pheasants were a frequent presence on the cottage grounds, and the many trees were alive with the comings and goings and singing and chirping of countless birds. At one point the Old Man, in a giddy mood, brought home a bantam rooster and a pair of bantam hens. The rooster soon exhausted the hens and presumably sought solace with any pheasant hen he could nail down, the observed result being at least one rather exotic-looking hybrid.

When you crossed the walkway from the thirteenth tee, you came to a small shelter erected over a well from which passersby could, by means of a tin cup hung on a nail in one of the shelter's posts, drink the most delicious water I've ever tasted. It was always cold, always refreshing. Later, when I started to caddy at National, I looked forward to it as does a desert nomad to an oasis.

It should have been a paradise to a boy, and in many respects it was, but the nearest house was almost a mile distant and I can't begin to describe my loneliness. My much-loved brother was away, and any parents of a twelve-year-old boy would be hard-pressed to fill the void. Mine tried, especially my mother, but still I was a lonely kid. I filled my nonschool hours riding my bicycle and exploring pretty much every square inch of the area within a half mile or so of the cottage. I used to look for and find bits of flint I convinced myself were Indian arrowheads, and I always was on the lookout for wild flowers, bunches of which I'd pick in shameless attempts to win my mother's approval.

As long as I did nothing to disturb or distract the golfers, the admonition being to remain quiet and stay out of sight as much as possible, I was allowed to fish in the ponds, especially the one in which there were perch. Any fish I caught were gutted on the spot and proudly trotted home and placed in the family refrigerator. Using a landing net and a length of string tied to a lure of gamey meat, I also went crabbing, quickly learning the stealth and dexterity required to half-fill a bucket with my lightning-fast quarry. These, too, I would take home so that my mother could cook them in boiling water as a preliminary to making a crab salad of which my father and I were big fans.

Despite its salinity, in winter the crab pond often froze over, and my father's work crew foreman, a man whose first name was Frank and whose last name I've forgotten, would cut a hole in the ice and, using a long pole to which was attached a multitined spear, probe the bottom mud for eels. If he was successful eels thus speared went into a gunnysack, and I remember staring at the heaving gunnysack as the captive creatures wriggled before expiring. It wasn't long before Frank brought me a smaller version of an eeling pole, and after he cut a hole in the ice for me, I too would probe for eels, sometimes with success, any I caught being added to his catch. I was afraid of snakes, and the eels were too close in resemblance for me to appreciate that they were fish. I never brought any home, and only as an adult did I discover that properly prepared they can be delicious.

One of the reasons my father's foreman probed for eels was his need to feed his family. Those were Depression days, and with the exception of the full-time mechanic, the work crew (the foreman included) were laid off from approximately the end of October, when the course closed, until mid-March, when it again opened for play. In the interim some of the men were lucky to find odd jobs or part-time work, but all of them had to scramble to provide for their families. Several kept chickens and most hunted and fished to put food on the table, all the while with fingers crossed that the Old Man would again hire them back come spring. My parents often answered a knock at the back door, there finding one of the crew or someone hoping to become one of the crew. Trying to make certain they would be favored, they would stand grinning with doffed cap in one hand and a chicken, a pheasant, a pair of wild ducks, or, more often than not, a big weak fish, a striped bass, or a big blue fish in the other. The seasonal legality of the taking of this bounty was never questioned; it was appreciated that the men were simply doing what they felt had to be done. Despite the men being told such supplications were unnecessary, the proffered provender was gratefully accepted.

The pond in which I went crabbing and eeling was also the pond over which golfers playing No. 14, a 336-yard par-4, had to hit their tee shots. When no one was in sight I regularly patrolled its edges, on the lookout for golf balls that had been hit into the water. When I saw one I thought I could reach, I'd run home and get my homemade retriever — a long bamboo pole at the limber end of which I had lashed an old tea strainer. Fishing out a submerged golf ball with this wobbly contrivance was no easy task, and any time I managed to land one I felt a rewarding sense of achievement. All such retrieved balls went into a string bag hung on a nail in one of the garages, seeing action only when I was moved to practice chipping on the lawn in back of the cottage.

Golf balls weren't the only things that splashed down in that pond. On a day in late April the Old Man's job-provided Model A Ford station wagon (upon which I learned to drive, incidentally) rolled into the cottage yard, its horn blowing briefly in what both my mother and I understood to be a summons. My mother went to the back door, and my father told her I should put on my swim trunks and come with him. When she asked what was afoot, he told her he had a little job he wanted me to do, that I'd be right back.

"You're not going to have him go swimming, are you?" she asked. "It's too cold."

In fact the day was sunny and warm, and I had been out and about in shorts and a polo shirt. Assured I wasn't going swimming, my mother relented; wearing my trunks, low-cut sneakers, and the polo shirt, I climbed up into the station wagon and off we went. Not far, as it turned out.

The Old Man stopped on the road near the fourteenth tee. Standing on it and peering down into the water were four golfers and their caddies. As we got out of the wagon and approached the tee, I began to get the picture—I was expected to wade into the water and retrieve whatever it was the others were looking for. The very idea chilled me, let alone the water. I had lived at National for a year and knew the water in nearby Peconic Bay didn't warm up enough for even teenage beach nuts until at least mid-May. But, my shirt removed and still wearing my sneakers, I was waved into the pond by parental command and told I was looking for a driver that had slipped from the hands of one of the golfers.

The water was icy-cold, shocking, numbing, and it took every smidgeon of whatever grit I possessed to wade out in it up to my waist, all the while responding to directions as to where, exactly, the submerged club might be. I felt along the bottom with my feet as I turned right or left when bidden, mindful that short weeks before, through a hole chopped in the ice, I had probed this very bottom for eels. At one point I was halted and told that was the spot, that I was to duck my head down into the water to try and see the club. Shivering in the numbing cold, I lowered my face to the surface and opened my eyes. I could see nothing, of course, and, gasping, reported accordingly. I was told to try a little to the right, then a little to the left, step back a bit, now step forward. Still nothing.

By this time I was truly chilled to the bone. Told to come out of the water, I left it at a far more brisk pace than I had entered it. I hopped around a bit and, still wet, donned my shirt. I continued to shiver as the man who had lost the driver thanked me for my effort, then went on his way with his fellow golfers and their caddies. I was told to run home and get into some dry clothes.

Upon seeing my soaked state as I came through the back door, my mother was outraged. She hustled me into a hot shower, then made certain I toweled myself off until I was completely dry. Minutes later I was in clean, dry clothes and my moccasins and out the door, off on missions known only to thirteen-year-old boys with time on their hands.

My mother's low opinion of the adventure was made known that evening the moment the Old Man stepped through the door. He was berated for risking my health in such a thoughtless way. What in the world did he have on his mind? How could he do such a thing? And so on. When at last she had had her say, my father said, "You know, that cheap s.o.b. didn't even tip the kid."

Later, seated at an atmospherically frosty dinner table, he

looked over at me, smiled, and winked. After all, we were co-conspirators and cognizant of the ways of men. Had he, at that moment, asked me to storm the Bastille single-handedly, I'd have done so.

I suffered nary a sneeze nor a sniffle, and the incident was filed away to be brought out and laughed about many years later, no laughter more rewarding than my own.

• **8** •

The Way It Was, Part I

WHILE IN COLLEGE and a not overly enthusiastic student of an economics course, I was introduced to the term "division of labor." I wasn't then (nor am I now) exactly certain what the term meant, but on the occasions I now see it in print or hear it referred to, I tend to think about the division of labor among the gang of men who worked under my father's supervision at National.

I can't at this point swear to the number, but I think the crew totaled twelve, maybe fourteen, including the foreman and the mechanic. Most of the men were of Polish extraction, one notable exception being a cheerful and voluble Italian named Mike Ambrose. The Old Man's work crew at Sunningdale had been comprised largely of Italian immigrants, and while my father spoke not a word of Polish, he had along the way picked up a smattering of Italian. Although Ambrose spoke more than passable English (he had served in the U.S.

Army in World War I), the Old Man and he often swapped thoughts or expressions in a tongue foreign to the other men, who may or may not have cared one way or another. But then they often spoke Polish among themselves, which to Ambrose and my father could have been Swahili. (However, largely through schoolmates who came from Polish-speaking homes, I did pick up a few Polish expressions, none of them polite.)

The foreman — the aforementioned Frank — was a big man, solidly built and very strong. He knew the work that had to be done, was dependable, and appeared to have the respect of the men over whom he held sway. He was always kind to me (teaching me to spear eels, for example), and to the best of my knowledge my father valued him. I liked him.

The mechanic was a testy wizard named Joe Onesko. Small and wiry, I rarely saw him without the stub of a cigarette centered on his lower lip. He wore gold wire-rimmed eyeglasses that sat perched about halfway down his nose. If there was one indispensable man in the operation, he was that man.

He could overhaul or repair anything, be it a massive water pump, a tractor transmission, a dump truck engine, a push mower, or the often balky conveyer through which the topsoil was blended and piled. He was a magician with a welding torch or a blacksmith's hammer and anvil, able to cobble together from metal scraps any improvised piece of equipment for which my father could provide only the sketchiest of sketches. The Old Man would dream up and make crude sketches of something he thought might solve a certain problem—a modification of a sod cutter, say—and the mechanic would make it. Beautifully, too. In his way he was an artist, and he knew it, which at times led to frank exchanges of views with my father.

Year-round his working days were spent administering to the golf course maintenance equipment. He was forever sharpening mower blades or adjusting their height, overhauling something, painting whatever needed painting, fussing over the various engines that powered the tractors and the trucks, crawling around the huge pistons of the water pumps, rewiring something, or repairing this or that. Without him or someone very much like him, maintenance of National's classic golf course might well have come to a halt.

Two of the men were assigned the job of mowing fairways. Most of their days were spent riding and steering tractors that pulled big six-unit gang mowers. I'd guess few such mowers are in use on today's golf courses, but once they were a staple in the inventory of course maintenance equipment. In appearance the individual units looked like giant versions of a typical reel-type push mower. I recall one unit being "in harness" immediately behind the towing tractor, two side-by-side behind the lead unit, and the other three side-by-side behind the first three. Combined, the mowers cut a swath that may have been as much as fifteen feet wide. The tractors moved along at a fairly brisk pace, too, meaning it didn't take overly long to mow a fairway. Nonetheless, it was an all-day job, and added to it was the mowing of the grounds around the clubhouse

Tractor-hauled gang mowers made short work of mowing fairways, in golf's earliest days a job left to sheep. If I was lucky, and if my father was off-premises, I got to ride along, occasionally even to steer. A sickle bar mowed the heavy roughs.
(Courtesy of Jacobsen, a Textron Company.)

and occasionally of the club's somewhat abbreviated practice range. The follow-up trimming of the clubhouse grounds, as well as the care and feeding of its flowers and the trimming of its shrubs, was yet another job performed by the Old Man's crew.

One of the two men assigned to fairway mowing duties was named Tony Zelinski, the other Lorillard Smith. Both at various times provided patient companionship and conversation to a lonely teenage boy.

Lorillard Smith was a Shinnecock Indian who lived on the tribe's reservation on the other side of neighboring Shinnecock Hills Golf Club, a past and future U.S. Open venue. To me Smith appeared to be a black man, but I was told he was a descendant of freed slaves who in the early to mid nineteenth century had intermarried with a number of Shinnecock women following the loss at sea of many of the tribe's men who crewed on whaling ships out of Sag Harbor. You can bet all of this had great appeal to me, and I looked upon him as I would a war-bonneted Plains chief. Occasionally when he was mowing the fairways and knew my father was off the premises, he'd let me ride with him on the tractor, even allowing me to steer. He was a gentle man who never talked down to me, and he patiently answered what I'm sure were my many questions.

I never rode on a mowing tractor with Tony Zelinski, but I spent many hours in his company during summer nights when he worked overtime watering the course. He, too, was a patient man, and it was through him I learned the basics of driving a car.

A typical day for the crew would start at 7 a.m., when mowers, rakes, shovels, bamboo poles, push brooms, sickles, scythes, and whatever else might be needed were loaded aboard two trucks. The men would then hoist themselves up, sit or stand wherever they could find room, and be driven to one of the holes to which they were assigned. Each man was

View from the elevated tee on No. 6 showing the green on No. 12 (*left*), the green on No. 13 (*center*), and (*right*) the thirteenth tee and the shelter of the well from which flowed the most delicious spring water imaginable. (Photo courtesy of the author.)

responsible for the greens, tees, bunkers, and surrounding areas of two or more holes, the hole assignments depending upon their proximity to each other. For example, the sixth tee and green were within short walking distance of the twelfth green and the thirteenth tee, and one man would be responsible for all these locations.

The first order of the day was to pole a green using a long

and whippy length of bamboo. This swept aside the morning dew and any overnight worm casts in preparation for the donkey work of mowing the green. The term "donkey work" is not ill-advised; pushing the T-handled greens mowers of seventy years ago was brutally hard work. For one thing they were heavy—so heavy that two men were required to load one on and off a truck, along with the dolly upon which it was wheeled from green to green. Their many-bladed reels were geared to spin at a considerably faster speed than their trailing roller drums, meaning there were just that many more moving parts the fellow doing the mowing had to set and keep in motion. Adding to the weight was a metal catch basket mounted in front of the whirring reel, and while only a mere fraction of grass was being mowed, the basket quickly filled and had to be emptied. As if pushing the wretched things wasn't hard enough, it was fussy, demanding work—all mow lines had to be straight, and any overlap on the aprons of the greens was almost a firing squad offence.

The catch basket was upended on a poncho-sized piece of canvas spread out at some spot off the green. When the canvas became full, its corners were gathered up and its contents carried to and dumped in an inconspicuous spot, usually in among some brush or in nearby woods. The process then was repeated until the entire green was mowed. And if a day or two of rain made daily mowing of the greens impossible, pushing one of the mowers over the considerably longer grass became ten miles of dirt road, every inch of it uphill. If rain continued for more than a day or two, the mowers were set higher for the initial postrain cut, then set lower to a height consistent with both a proper putting surface and with the well-being of the green's turf.

Once the greens were tended to, attention was paid to the tees, the men mowing them at one height and mowing the areas around them at a slightly loftier height. Tee mowing required a different mower, one not unlike a reel mower once common to every household garage but heavier. Setting the different heights required a turn or two of an adjustment screw at both ends of the reel. Here again lines had to be straight, the demarcation between tee surface and surrounding area made plain to see. The cut grass was collected and made inconspicuous in much the same manner as were the clippings from greens.

In the course of driving from hole to hole on his daily inspection rounds, the Old Man would, after looking over a tee's surface and noting worn and unworn areas, set the markers — at National, I recall, they were (and still may be) red for championship, dark green for regular, and white for short. The term "ladies tees" was uttered rarely if ever; women were allowed on the course only one day during a week and, while I'm not sure about this, perhaps also on Sundays after 11 a.m.

Another chore involved hand-raking the bunkers with big wooden rakes and trimming their borders with a sickle and a step-on edger. The Old Man liked to see properly prepared bunkers, all rake tine lines parallel, no shaggy edges. Most greens had at least one and often two or more bunkers, some of them quite large, and there were no such things as riding machines to do it, so raking the bunkers was a time-consuming job. Also, any fairway bunkers had to be raked as well. On occasion I was set to the chore and can promise you that after an hour or two of fussily raking sand under a broiling sun, you can start imagining yourself to be Beau Geste on work detail at Fort Zinderneuf.

Ball washers were another thing that had to be attended to—filled to an appropriate level with water, cleanser added, opposing scrub brushes checked for wear, attached cream-colored towel looked at to make certain it was reasonably clean.

It's numbing to think of someone seeing in his mind's eye multiple acres of immaculate, but that's what the Old Man liked to picture. A golf course in absolutely perfect condition was an impossible goal, but that never deterred him from pursuing it. Don't misunderstand; the goal wasn't the precisely groomed and fussed-over courses of today's PGA and LPGA tours, especially Augusta National in Georgia, with its crosshatched fairway mowing patterns and artfully planted azaleas. Such would have been beyond his imagination. He would have deemed it artificial. Having grown up in St. Andrews and having thought of the Old Course as definitive, he wanted his golf course to blend seamlessly into the land and surroundings upon which it was built, to look as if it had been in place since time immemorial. On a golf course, then, daisies and black-eyed Susans belonged, azaleas did not.

• 9 •

Off Limits

FROM THE FRONT, the main part of the clubhouse at National was and still is an impressive pile that might suggest a manorial home in Great Britain, or perhaps a British municipal building. Were it hugging a horizon in rural Yorkshire, it would be right at home. And if you saw it on a street in, say, Manchester, Leeds, or Glasgow, you might assume it housed some sort of ministry or council.

My memories of its interior are vague, probably because it was forbidden territory by edict of my father, even if extended the opportunity to have a look around. I recall seeing only the big kitchen, a dining room that looked out over Great Peconic Bay, and a big room I later would think of as being typical of a proper men's club, back when the term implied massive chairs covered in dark leather, library tables and reading lamps, big fireplaces, big ashtrays, Webster Fancy Tail cigars, and card tables covered in green felt. (These days the implication of the

No swimming pool, no tennis courts, no cocktail lounge, no
frills: National's clubhouse overlooks Great Peconic Bay and is as
purposeful as a baseball bat. For decades the club's venerable dining room has been widely and justly famous for its lobster salad.
(Photo courtesy of the author.)

term "men's club" may be summed up by a restaurant marquee I once observed on La Cienega Boulevard in Los Angeles:
"Total Nudity from 12 Noon.") On an upper floor were overnight accommodations for members and guests, and on a still
higher floor were rooms for the live-in help—some kitchen
staff, chambermaids, maybe the locker room attendant, and
so on.

Present in the clubhouse six days a week was the book-keeper, a quietly dressed and gentle man named Ernest Herring, an Englishman who lived "off campus" in Southampton. (In 1946 he began a twenty-one-year career as the club's manager, and his son, Randall, succeeded him as manager in 1968.) Although there may have been, I can't recall the presence of a secretary or of any clerical help.

Presiding in every sense of the word over this considerable enterprise was a formidable Englishman named James Ellis. A tall, big-boned man with impressive gray hair who also lived "off campus," he was given to wearing tweed knickers, a matching tweed jacket and buttoned-up vest, a tweed cap, a buttoned-up white shirt and quiet tie, ribbed tan woolen hose, and dark brown kiltie shoes that appeared to weigh a ton (at least that's what he was wearing whenever I saw him). He was the essence of dignity and decorum; the only time he was without a suit jacket was when he was in his rolled-up shirtsleeves tending a small vegetable and herb garden he had planted in back of the garage that among other things housed the club's "go fer" Plymouth station wagon. This was in 1938, and he had been the club's manager since its clubhouse opened in 1912.

Based on overheard conversations between my parents, I understood that the staff both revered and feared the man, the former because his supervision of the club's day-to-day routine was confident and just, the latter because . . . well, he had a problem. Every so often he'd go off on a bat. He'd be sober for months, even as long as a year or more, then like Jekyll and Hyde he'd turn into a roaring drunk. The descent was well-known to the staff. The storm warning would be a sudden bottle of beer with his lunch. On day two of the approaching storm he'd have a cocktail before lunch. The storm would break on day three, when he'd have both a cocktail *and* a bottle of beer, its fury increasing with each succeeding drink. His toots would last for days, perhaps even a week or more, during which the staff did its best to keep a low profile. Fortunately he seemed always to have the presence of mind to remain in and around the club's big kitchen. Eventually the storm's fury would be spent (occasionally in "dry out" facilities at the Southampton Hospital), and things would go on as they always had, the hallmark being superb and discreet service.

Mr. Ellis—always "Mr. Ellis" to my father, to other employees of the club, and very likely to most of its members—was driven to and from the clubhouse by the club's driver, a cheerful man named Eddie O'Kunewicz, whose brother, Joe, was National's caddymaster. It was Eddie who would "go fer" the mail and for whatever was needed by way of clubhouse supplies, and it was he who picked up members or their guests at the Southampton railroad station and shuttled them to and from the clubhouse. On occasion, knowing Eddie was going into town, my mother would call him and ask that he stop by the cottage so that he might pick up something for her. Often at such times he would ask me if I wanted to go along, invitations I eagerly accepted. As much as I enjoyed roaming around National, I was hungry to see other places, other people. I always remained in the station wagon while he went about his errands, but all the while I was a shameless rubberneck, making it a point to take in everything I could.

One night at the dinner table during my father's second year at National, he said, "Well, they're bringing the Old Man home." I listened (remember, this was a time when children were seen and not heard) and soon realized the reference was to National's laird, Charles Blair Macdonald. According to the discussion that ensued, he had been in Florida for the winter, was desperately ill, and wanted to see his beloved golf course and clubhouse one more time before checking out. I understood he would arrive the next day at the railroad station and would be taken by ambulance to the clubhouse.

I listened to the details of the arrangement carefully and made the decision to at least see the ambulance as it drove by, perhaps even catch a glimpse of its almost mythical passenger. Accordingly, I hopped on my bicycle on the appointed day and stationed myself along the public road separating the shallow bay from one of the ponds (the one into which, earlier that spring, I had waded in a vain attempt to find a driver that had slipped from a golfer's hands).

You have to understand that Charles Blair Macdonald had been a big noise in American golf and was in fact its first national amateur champion. A big man, strong, vain, and imperious, he brooked no criticism — he was right, right every time, and if you didn't believe it you had only to ask him. A Chicagoan made confident by a considerable personal fortune, he had been a student at the University of St. Andrews, where he learned to play golf and where he rubbed elbows with several lions of the game, among them Old Tom Morris and his spectacularly skilled son, three-time consecutive British Open Champion Tom Morris Jr. The exposure and the experience made Macdonald a golfing zealot, and he returned home determined not only to launch but to dominate golf in the United States.

He soon became the American game's sword-rattler, riding roughshod over all those whose opinions were contrary to his own. As the late Herbert Warren Wind, one-time dean of American golf writers, put it, "There were only two ways to take Macdonald. Either you liked him intensely or you disliked him intensely. There was no middle ground." In designing and building National, however, this far from cuddly man gave America its first classic golf course.

All this was known and discussed in my household, especially when in the spring of 1939 it was learned he was being brought back to National to die.

At any rate I waited a good two hours before, at last, I spotted the approaching ambulance. It rushed by me in a blur. I couldn't see anything, only the ambulance and its driver, and couldn't swear to much other than that I was one of the last to be, in a way, in the man's presence, however fleetingly and however indirectly. But ever since, when I come across his name in some golf-related reading, I think back to that day and of almost seeing Charles Blair Macdonald. I mean, you know, there I was. Sort of, anyway.

A few days later I learned he had been taken, again by ambulance, from the clubhouse to the hospital in Southampton, where he died. The date was April 21, 1939. He was eighty-three years old.

The head waiter (and later Mr. Ellis's successor as manager at National) was a man named Martin Wobst. He may have been a naturalized American, but he was definitely a pro-German German, and considering what was happening in Europe at the time not in the Top Ten on our household's hit parade. As accounts of Germany's diplomatic muscling and smashing military victories appeared time and again in the newspapers and were reported over the radio, Wobst had the annoying habit of gloating. My Scottish father, who had served in the Black Watch as a young man and in the U.S. Army in France during World War I, wore his enemies openly, and heading the list were Germans, especially gloating Germans. In fact, while at Sunningdale years before he and the chef, a German named Lambert, somehow managed to get into it, the result being a chef with a very sore jaw and a couple of loose teeth and my father the object of a visit by an amused Town of Greenburg policeman. Any exchanges between Wobst, who remained National's manager throughout the war, and the Old Man tended to be minimal.

Not so with the club's golf professional, however, a fellow Scotsman named Alick Gerard with whom my father spent a lot of time (perhaps to his ultimate detriment, as it turned out). A muffin-faced man with a ruddy complexion, Gerard, originally from Aberdeen, had been National's professional since 1930 and was well-entrenched in the position and with the club's membership, all of whom he knew and addressed by name. Very much of the old school, I never saw him without a white shirt buttoned at the collar, necktie in place, its tails tucked into the front of the shirt, or without a cap. He had an easy, smooth, loosey-goosey swing that seemed as effortless as breathing, and while he was no shakes for distance off the tee, he was accurate with his long irons and had a dead-on short game.

I don't recall that he had an assistant. However, his son, Alick Gerard Jr., may have filled that position later on, for in the late 1940s he succeeded his father as National's professional. At the time, though, the younger Gerard, an accomplished golfer, was the assistant pro at Maidstone in nearby East Hampton. In winter the Gerards were the pro and assistant pro at the exclusive Mountain Lake Club in Lake Wales, Florida.

While there was no assistant pro, there was, most decidedly, a caddymaster, a muscular blond giant (or so he seemed to me) named Joe O'Kunewicz, who in ways both direct and indirect played a large part in my adolescence. As such he rates a chapter of his own because in today's business of golf—and never forget it *is* a bottom-line business—it's doubtful anyone like him even exists.

An Authentic Master

HE CALLED ME BILLY, I called him Joe. When his name came up in our household the reference always was to "Joe Oakey." He was, as mentioned, tall and very blond, his hair always in a crew cut. I was in awe of him, not only because of his impressive size but because of the things he could do—plus he had, and was generous with, the sunniest of smiles. He was only a couple of years older than my brother and therefore in my fuzzy perception a sort of quasi-contemporary. Any Navy leave my brother had always included at least one round of golf with Joe Oakey.

He could drive a golf ball from the regular tee on No. 1 at National to the green, a slight dogleg left, a distance of over three hundred yards. Alick Gerard, National's professional, often would have Joe demonstrate this ability to skeptics, usually some member's guest who, playing the course for the first time, expressed being intimidated by its overall length (just under 6,500 yards from the regular tees, in those days considered a rather long course). Gerard would scoff at such carps, saying his caddymaster could drive the first green. When doubt was expressed Joe would be told to get his driver and show the man how it was done. Strong and athletic, Joe would tee it up and let fly with his powerful swing, the result usually being just as advertised. A headwind might knock the ball down a few yards short of the green, but an equal tailwind would send it flying over the back. When he actually played there's no telling how many times over the years he must have birdied that first hole.

I first got to know him during the off-season. When in the late fall the course was closed and Alick Gerard headed for Florida, Joe, like the men in my father's crew, was cast adrift until the following spring. Fortunately, he was married to a part-time school teacher — while paid the pittance school teachers received, her income at least enabled the couple to scrape by. And like the men in the Old Man's gang, Joe hunted and fished and speared eels and dug clams.

On one memorable late fall occasion my father observed a flock of migrating Canadian geese landing on National's practice range, which was parallel to a stretch of the Great Peconic Bay shoreline. Word was passed to Joe, who raced home to get his shotgun and then out to the practice range, where, following a stealthy approach, with two shots he brought down two of the geese. Whether or not there was an open hunting season for the geese, I don't know, but my memory of the event is that it was illegal. I do know that my mother had to dig into her Fannie Farmer cookbook to learn how to roast a goose.

Word of the geese landing was passed to Joe because at the time he was refinishing a small library table for my mother, one of the off-season odd jobs he did for my family whenever either my father or my mother had something for him to do. (One of his least enviable jobs, surely, was teaching my mother to drive the family's floor-shift 1936 Dodge sedan.) The refinishing was being done in the cottage's living room, a protective tarpaulin spread out on the floor, and I made it my business to watch the entire procedure. He always told me what he was doing and why, which years later served me well when I refinished some furniture on my own. I remember him rubbing in coat after coat of linseed oil, and he did a marvelous job on the table, turning what had been a somewhat tired piece into a thing of rich beauty. I think it's now owned by one of my nieces.

Had I known it at the time, I would have appreciated his craftsmanship even more, for even though a young man he was a master maker of the woods that bore Alick Gerard's imprint. They, too, were things of beauty, the heads a glistening reddish brown, the finish dimensional to the point where it appeared you could probe its depth with a finger. He made them on a small workbench that was on one side of the bag room in what was (and for all I know still may be) National's modest, no-nonsense golf shop.

The raw makings of the heads for the woods were stored on

a bag room rack in a big corrugated cardboard shipping carton. Also stored on the rack were hickory replacement shafts, for at the time the transition from hickory to steel shafts was still an on-going though waning thing, and it was not uncommon over the course of a season for a golfer to break one or more of the wooden shafts. I don't know who supplied them, but the heads for the woods arrived as squareish blocks of persimmon, the one concession to their eventual use being that what would be the necks of the clubs were roughly formed. From such crude beginnings Joe could and would produce works of art.

Whoever had taught him, possibly Gerard himself, taught him well. Clamping one of the blocks in a vise, the jaws of which were padded, Joe would have at it with a variety of wood rasps, soon transforming it into the rough shape of whatever club was on order. Usually he made matched sets of woods, two or three of which were on display in the front part of the strictly utilitarian golf shop. But most of the sets were custom-made, more often than not for members. Occasionally a golfer would want just a new driver, a new brassie, or a new spoon.

I use the terms "brassie," a 2-wood, and "spoon," a 3-wood, because that's what they were called. The soles of the clubs were indeed stamped with the appropriate number, but the common names for them were brassie and spoon. A 5-wood was called a cleek, a nineteenth-century term once applied to certain irons. In 1939, however, I recall such clubs as being rather rare, as were clubs called jiggers, short-shafted slightly lofted irons intended mainly for delicate pitch-and-run work around greens. Although numbered sets of matched irons were available, many golf bags at the time included a mid-iron (roughly a 3-iron), a mashie (a 5-iron), a mashie-niblick (a 7-iron), and a niblick (about a 9-iron). Putters were either blades or semi-mallet-headed clubs known as "Schenectady" putters.

Once the wooden clubhead had been roughly formed, Joe would begin its fine-tuning. First using what appeared to be a comparatively fine-toothed rasp, with gentle touches he would shape the clubhead consistent with its intended use — a larger and only slightly lofted face for a driver, marginally smaller and with a more lofted face for a brassie, smaller still and even more lofted for a spoon. A hole was drilled from the top of the clubhead's neck through to its heel to accommodate the shaft. The neck was then carefully tapered so that when finished it and the shaft would appear to be a single unit. Then he'd begin the delicate and seemingly endless business of sanding, first with relatively coarse sandpaper and eventually with sandpaper so fine it felt almost slick to the touch. To the best of my knowledge he had no pattern to go by; it was all eyeball and experience. The final smoothing was done with very fine steel wool.

If so ordered, another step in the process involved carefully cutting a top-to-sole dovetail in the face of the club, into which a tapered or mortised piece of ram's horn or some similar material was fitted and glued. This was known as an insert, its purpose being to absorb the shock of impact with the ball. Then, using a special rasp, the face of the clubhead was scored in a crosshatch pattern. This laborious handcrafting process would result in an almost white clubhead of classic shape and size, including appropriate bulge and roll.

The next step involved seating and gluing the steel shaft in the neck of the clubhead. The shafts were made by True Temper and were available in two flexes, standard ("regular") and "whippy," the latter lighter in weight thanks to its thinner wall. The shaft was inserted the entire length of the neck through to the sole, its round open end then plugged with an inch or so of appropriately sized and glued dowel. Once clubhead and shaft were united, Joe would ready a dish (no more than a saucer, really) of stain, dip a bit of rag into it as a brush, and, being careful to work around its face, stain the clubhead the above-mentioned reddish brown. I can't remember whether or not multiple coats of stain were needed, but when the clubhead was dry, he'd tightly wind about an inch and a half of the tapered neck and an inch and a half of the shaft with a single spiral of heavy-duty black carpet thread and then tie it off. This was called "whipping," its purpose being to reinforce the point at which the tapered neck and shaft were joined.

All this done, Joe would then "build" a gradually tapered foundation grip using felt tape and gauze bandage tape, the final result wrapped in a leather tape spiral and "whipped" top and bottom with black carpet thread. Then, using a special punch, a hammer, and a strip of golf leaf, he'd carefully impress

Alick Gerard

National Golf Links

on top of the clubhead. He'd use another punch to impress on the sole of the club the number appropriate to its use—driver, brassie, spoon, or cleek.

The final and to my young eyes most appealing touch was the application to the clubhead and its whipping multiple coats of clear and fragrant lacquer. Applied with a brush with long and supple bristles, the lacquer was stroked on smoothly and evenly; suddenly what had all along been a work in progress became a finished thing of beauty and, literally, a joy not only to behold but to hold.

Although it's almost inconceivable in these days of assembly line–produced $500 technological wonder rods, the gorgeous handmade woods sold for about $30 each, a matched set of three for less than $100.

Also a thing of the past is the ambiance of the place in which they were made—a mix of green-shaded bare-bulb light and sunlight pouring through a pair of windows that needed washing, a well-worn and cluttered workbench, and the distinctive smells of leather, glue, and lacquer. Permeating all of it was the skill and dedication of the man whose special place it was.

Joe Oakey was named head professional at National in 1956, a job he held until retirement in 1981. But like the proverbial old fire horse, he couldn't stay away from the shop that had been his home-away-from-home for almost fifty years. Accompanied by his dog, he regularly showed up to hang around and pass the time of day. I last saw him during a visit to National in the late 1990s. He called me Billy.

· 11 ·

A Picasso I Never Was

THE TEE MARKERS AT NATIONAL were wooden balls about the size of a large croquet ball into which a six-inch steel spike had been glued. They were put out when the course opened in the spring and were brought in when it closed in the fall. Their subsequent piling on the concrete floor of an unheated room at the maintenance barn blew a numbing wind through my teenage heart. One of my over-the-winter jobs was to paint them and I dreaded it, mainly because I wasn't very good at it.

Paint and the brushes with which it's applied have always presented a formidable challenge to me. Paint, regardless of the container in which it is held, for some reason has always demonstrated a maddening tendency to tip over, while paint brushes seem to fly out of my hand at inopportune moments. Besides, my father was a stickler, and even though painting a wooden ball is about as complex as breathing, I seemed unable to do the job to his satisfaction.

The balls painted bright red marked the championship tees, those painted dark green the regular tees, and those painted white the short tees. From the reds the course measured a little over 6,800 yards, from the greens a little over 6,400 yards, and from the short tees a fraction over 5,800 yards. National was, really, the nation's first long course. Including the back-ups for each color, I was required to paint 123 markers—41 of them red, 41 dark green, and 41 white. Had I not been what my father at times referred to as bone-lazy, I suppose I could have polished them off in a day. But because I hated the chore and because avoiding work if at all possible was a matter of teenage pride, painting those wooden balls seemed to take forever.

First I had to go over each one with a wire brush to remove dried mud and loose paint, and then over each spike to remove any rust or dirt. It was a dusty job during which I sneezed a lot and somehow managed to become absolutely filthy. Then I had to wipe each marker down with a cloth soaked in turpentine and line it up on a plank elevated between two cement building blocks and into which holes had been drilled to accommodate the spikes. The actual painting of each marker was simple—hold it upside down by its spike, paint the bottom around the base of the spike, put the brush down, grasp the marker by its upper half, and set it right-side-up in one of the holes drilled in the plank. That done, only minimal talent was required to paint the sides and top of each one. Although I certainly qualified on the "minimal talent" requirement, I couldn't seem to do the job to my father's satisfaction—I used too much paint, I didn't use enough paint, I missed spots, I was too slow . . . whatever. To this day I can hear it all in my head.

The real hazard, however, was the paint itself . . . and the brushes. I seemed to get an awful lot of the former on the floor and on my hands and clothes, and it seemed I never did do a proper job of cleaning the latter. But a genuine catastrophe with which I became all too familiar was an upended can of paint, its red, white, or dark-green brilliance spreading on the concrete floor while the one who spilled it — me — wondered whether it was preferable to die by putting a revolver to my head or by simply washing out to sea with the tide. The inevitable alternative to either choice was a paternal eruption during which my clumsiness was certain to be given thorough and repeated emphasis, thus making the revolver or the fatal swim seem almost attractive. Worse, of course, was that after the Old Man's wrath was spent I'd be ordered to clean up the mess, which meant being down on my hands and knees and a lot of wiping with rags and scrubbing with turpentine.

This sort of thing tended to make the days long, especially in November in a drafty, chilly barn. My waiting bicycle and the freedom it represented called to me loud and clear, but to no avail; the markers had to be painted, it was my job to do so, and that was that. But in the spring and summer months to come, during which I occasionally caddied, I'd take note of the shiny, freshly painted tee markers and feel the nudge of quiet pride that goes with doing a pretty good job. After all, the tee markers *were* out there, and I really *did* paint them. I remember once mentioning my having done so to a man for whom I was caddying. He ignored me.

Another job for which I was occasionally tapped was to "help Tony with the watering." In contrast to painting tee markers, this was a plum assignment. For one thing it meant being out and about on summer nights when the air was clear and cool and the sky was alive with stars. For another it meant being cooled now and then in the spray of the sprinklers. What I had in mind, however, was that helping with the watering meant I might, just might, get a chance to drive the tractor; like most kids my age I was hot for the years to fly by so I'd be old enough (sixteen) to qualify for an official New York State learner driver's permit. What my mother had in mind was that I didn't get soaked to the skin and come down with a cold, or be bitten to death by mosquitoes.

The tractor was really a sort of scaled-down pickup. It was called a Roseman, its principal feature being a 1938 Ford pickup truck chassis upon which had been mounted a single bench seat and a boxlike wooden body into which hose and sprinklers were loaded. There was no cab, no windshield, just the box and the bench seat. It was powered by a much-geared-down Ford v8 engine, its top speed being maybe twenty-five miles-per-hour. But it had a dash-mounted electric starter button and a floor-mounted shift lever, its three-speed gearbox engaged by means of a standard "H" pattern. In first gear it crawled but probably could have pulled down a house. In second gear it wasn't much faster. Even so, when in third gear and behind the wheel of this comparative tortoise, I was Wilbur Shaw on the backstretch at Indy.

There were two categories of watering: the greens and perhaps the tees and surrounding areas, and the fairways, the contrast between the two like night and day. I don't recall both ever being done on the same night.

Watering a green involved setting up a wheel sprinkler at a point at which most of the green's area would be covered by a slowly rotating sprinkler head. Reasonably near each green was an open box placed below ground level, at the dirt bottom of which could be found a sprinkler and a coiled length or two of standard-gauge garden hose. The hose had to be dragged out, the sprinkler attached to its business end, then placed on the green for maximum coverage. I recall National's greens as being fairly large, and often it was necessary to change the location of the sprinkler two or three times over the course of a night's watering. This constant checking of the sprinklers meant a lot of driving to and fro on the golf course's dirt roads, and being on private property there was no officialdom to question the age of the Roseman's fearless driver.

I don't know when National's irrigation system was laid out, but it was probably when the course was built. The system was pressurized by two electrically powered pumps, one of which was massive (in my eyes, anyway), both located in the maintenance barn complex. The water came from underground wells, and like the water in the spring at the end of the walkway on No. 13, it was always cold and delicious. On nights when the Old Man decided watering was called for, the mechanic had to be on overtime duty to start, keep lubricated, and generally attend the pumps. Usually only the big pump — an all-black behemoth made by Worthington — was required to keep the system suitably pressurized. I always looked forward to its switch being thrown; there'd be a whine of its big electric motor, then its big pistons would start in motion, awesome in their power and deafening in their steady *ka-lunk, ka-lunk, ka-lunk* rhythm.

Keep in mind all this watering business was very much a hands-on operation. There was no computerized irrigation system, no in-ground pop-up sprinkler heads (not at National, anyway), no automatic timers, no control panel making possible selective watering at any point on the golf course. This was labor-intensive donkey work, pleasant donkey work to be sure, but a few hours of dragging hoses here and there, coiling them back into their storage boxes, and hooking up and unhooking dozens of sprinklers could be tiring.

Although called upon occasionally to coil or drag hoses, my main job on such nights was to man the taps, that is, to turn the water on and off at Tony's direction. He, and I, if I was lucky, would drive the tractor to a point near whatever was being watered — a green or a tee area — and the two of us would spring into action, Tony to the sprinkler and me to the in-use tap. It got to be a routine requiring no instruction other than a request to turn the water off and, after a wait while he repositioned a sprinkler, a request to turn the water back on. When he was satisfied with the sprinkler's coverage pattern, we'd hop back on the Roseman and go on to the next hole upon which a green or tee was being watered.

He graciously acknowledged my assistance; as I think about it, I probably saved him a lot of walking back and forth. As for me, I was always happy to crawl into bed after a few hours of "help(ing) Tony with the watering."

• **12** •

The Really Hard Stuff

EXCEPT FOR FARMERS and maybe airline pilots, no one sweats weather like a golf course superintendent. If the profession has a motto it has to be: "Moderation in all things."

A typical superintendent lives and dies with rainfall or the lack thereof. A sudden cold snap can snuff out struggling shoots of newly seeded grass, or literally nip in the bud any decorative planting for which he has high hopes. An all-day high, dry wind can parch all but the hardiest greenery. Fog can roll in and bring with it one or more blights that can kill or damage the tender, closely cropped grass of putting surfaces. A prolonged dry spell can bring with it a proliferation of certain turf-damaging insects. Prolonged rainfall, in addition to drowning turf grass in low-lying areas, can bring out still other insects. The process overall, then, is one of tinkering, of adjusting, of fine-tuning, much as auto mechanics before the advent of fuel injectors had to tune carburetors.

The Old Man sweat the rain, and the lack of it made him edgy. At such times when he'd come home at the end of the day and my mother would ask how things went, he'd say, "Okay, only damnit, we need rain." He was a familiar caller to the local U.S. Coast Guard station, back then about the only semireliable source of what sort of weather might be expected. I say "semireliable" because even though he called regularly, he believed only about half of what he was told; he seemed to rely as much on his instincts as he did on official weather reports. He habitually listened to morning, noon, and evening radio news broadcasts, his interest equally divided between what was going on in the world and the maddeningly sketchy summaries of weather possibilities. Our family regularly listened to and enjoyed a long-gone weekly radio program called *Fibber McGee and Molly*. The character Fibber often referred to his local weatherman as "Ol' Probability." Hearing that reference, my father would comment that McGee was right on the money.

Pop always claimed he could smell the approach of rain hours before clouds began to gather and darken the sky. He'd step out the door in the morning, scan the sky, sniff, and say either, "No rain today" or, "We may get some rain this afternoon." My mother had great faith in these pronouncements, fearlessly hanging out the family washing if he said there'd be no rain, hanging it on clotheslines strung in the cottage basement if he said there would be. Rarely was she crossed up.

Apart from the greens (over which he fussed more, I'm

sure, than he fussed over me as a goo-gooing infant), his great concerns were the fairways; seeing them go off-color under a hot summer sun or during a period of drought was an affront he took personally. As dry, hot day after dry, hot day went by he'd become increasingly edgy, his uplifted eyes forever searching the skies for a sign of approaching rain clouds. When at last he felt himself cornered with no way out, he'd order the fairways watered, which was no small undertaking, and me to "help Tony with the watering." Again, there was no computerized underground irrigation system, no computer-controlled pop-up sprinkler heads. Watering National's fairways back then was a slog involving massive, heavy sprinklers fed by two-and-a-half-inch woven fire hose.

Each fairway sprinkler consisted of a rotating arm mounted on a four-wheel hand truck pulled or pushed by means of a T-handle. The rotating arm was predominantly brass, the nozzles at each end I remember as being almost as big as a man's forearm. The upright base upon which the arm turned was an iron casting. The base of the hand truck, which measured maybe five feet long, two to three feet wide, and two inches thick, was fashioned of hardwood, its four edges protected by a steel side railing. The truck's wheels, about eight inches in diameter, were made of steel—no tires, just steel spokes and rims. The thing weighed a ton, especially to a teenage boy.

Only marginally lighter in weight were the rolls of fire hose used to connect these monsters to the nearest source of water. This exercise often involved rolling out and coupling two or more fifty-foot lengths of hose. During the course of an evening's watering, the woven cotton covering would become soaking wet, adding to the weight. Hard on thoughtless and unlucky hands were the hoses' heavy brass couplings; once hooked up, they were tightened with a special wrench not unknown to fly from one's hands, tearing a fingernail or nicking a knuckle. On nights when "help(ing) Tony with the watering" meant watering the fairways, it was an odds-on bet my blood would be drawn.

The sprinklers covered a circle as much as a hundred yards in diameter. Their spray majestic, launched into the air at a high angle and spewing out in a graceful arc, they were all power, and under a bright full moon the spray seemed almost ethereal. Keeping them pressurized involved starting up the second pump, smaller than the big Worthington but still an impressive mechanism. With both pumps going full tilt, the noise in the pump house was not unlike what you might expect to encounter in a foundry. You had to shout to be heard, even outside when the pump house doors were opened for ventilation. For all the noise, the pump house was a beacon in the night, its lights welcoming and somehow reassuring.

The actual fairway watering was, as might be imagined, out-and-out grunt work. The method was the same as that used to water the greens and tee areas — position the sprinklers for maximum coverage. In that most of the fairways were hundreds of yards in length, this could mean relocating the sprinklers three or more times. Late in the afternoon the sprinklers and needed hose were loaded aboard a truck for distribution to the fairways to be watered. Once they were off-loaded, moving them meant grabbing the T-handle and pulling or pushing one's guts out. I wasn't anywhere near strong enough to pull both sprinkler and hose. Tony was and did. But I could uncouple, roll up, and lug lengths of soaking-wet hose, the experience engraving on my mind forever respect for the strength of firefighters.

An evening's fairway watering would start around sundown and continue through until about midnight. Working in the dark required carrying a flashlight, which, in addition to illuminating whatever it was I was called upon to do, enabled me to spot a variety of wildlife. Rabbits were a common sight, as were field mice and the occasional rat. A now-and-then treat was to point my flashlight's beam at some perceived noise—a rustle among some bushes, say—and find looking back at me the reflected red lights of a deer's eyes. Deer weren't then and still aren't desirable neighbors for a golf course (their sharp hooves can raise hob with a putting surface or a raked sand trap), so upon spotting one I'd make a mad, hollering run at it, feeling strangely empowered when it scampered off out of sight.

At the time on Long Island only seasonal bow-and-arrow hunting for deer was allowed; hunting deer with any type of gun was forbidden. The one exception of which I was aware was my father, who officially was permitted to dispatch any deer caught damaging any part of the golf course or its grounds. This was a joke in our house, the Old Man not having the heart to do anything other than sound his piercing whistle to scare off any trespassing deer. In fact, the only critter I ever saw him kill was a big milk snake that had the misfortune to be found in a flower bed just outside the front door of our house at Sunningdale. Employing a proper Vardon overlap grip, the Old Man dispatched the snake with a few strokes of a mashie-niblick.

A common just-before-dark sight on watering evenings were pheasants, usually spotted near underbrush along the far edges of the roughs. The hens appeared dull, but the cocks were magnificent, colorful creatures that seemed to be nothing less than absolute monarchs. I always fancied myself bringing one down (shooting hens was forbidden) and proudly taking it home as provender for the table. But when one Christmas my brother gave me a new Savage single-barreled 20-gauge shotgun, there didn't appear to be a cock pheasant within forty miles. As a budding Nimrod I had to be content with doing my futile best to wipe out the entire rabbit population of Long Island's South Fork.

My forays with the shotgun were never very successful. Thinking back I realize the principles of stealth somehow eluded me. Instead of working my way quietly through the underbrush and in among the trees of the nearby woods, I preferred to walk along the open roughs, one eye out for possible game, the other for approaching golfers and maybe lost golf balls. If golfers were spotted I'd try to duck out of sight, the noise of my suddenly crashing into the underbrush shattering any hopes of coming across critters unaware of my approach. Besides, I had to encounter a critter that would stand reasonably still because I was required to ration my shots. Upon my expressing a desire to hunt rabbits, say, my mother would dole out perhaps a half dozen shells along with a cautionary lecture on the safe use of firearms. There were times when I'd return home with all six of the shells still in my jacket pocket; I hadn't seen a thing to shoot at, not even a bottle or a tin can. However, also in a pocket of my jacket I may have had two or three golf balls found in the roughs or under some scrub growth. It rarely was a total loss.

Other creatures occasionally encountered on watering nights were snakes. I'd come across them slithering through tall grass or curled up in a corner of a below-ground-level box in which a length or two of garden hose was coiled. Snakes terrified me, even harmless garter snakes. Their benefit to the environment in general and to the golf course in particular was explained in detail (for one thing, I was assured they held down the field mouse population), but these explanations fell on deaf ears. I wanted no part of snakes, nor, it seemed, did they of me. The speed with which they made their getaway I thought impressive, and I doubt I could have caught one even had I wanted to. Instead, I was happy and relieved to see them on their way.

One night, however, a dilemma presented itself.

Somehow an errant shot or an odd bounce had resulted in

a golf ball resting in a greenside hose box in which a snake also was taking its ease. I wanted the ball but equally wanted nothing to do with the snake. I considered getting a stick and trying to rout it out, but even that prospect lacked appeal. I took my problem to the ever-patient Tony, who walked over to the box, reached in, grabbed the snake by its tail, and flung it into some nearby tall grass. He said not a word but went back to the business of positioning a sprinkler. Sheepishly, I pocketed the ball and walked back to the waiting tractor. He didn't let me drive, and that night, when we were finished watering and I rode my bicycle home in the moonlight, I felt a little less than complete.

Tote That Bag, Watch That Ball

I WAS NEVER A REGULAR CADDY at National, my services usually being called upon when not enough caddies showed up to accommodate the day's golfers. At such times my father would drive me to the golf shop, and then I'd walk down to what was known as the caddy yard. At the time, the yard and its shed were some fifty or so yards in back of the shop. Needed caddies were summoned by name hollered from the first tee by the caddymaster. Premier bags — the bags of the best golfers or of those golfers known to be liberal tippers — went to the senior caddies, a number of whom were between-semester college students. The unemployed caddies, usually younger, less experienced, and less burly, passed time playing cards, pitching pennies, shooting craps, eating their often meager lunches, or playing cutthroat pitch-'n'-putt on the yard's bare ground with found balls and an old mid-iron that served as one of the shed's few amenities. Not being one of the regulars as well as being the greenkeeper's son made me an outsider. Although I was never threatened physically or verbally, the others talked around me, and I never was certain of what was afoot. I wasn't a cardplayer and didn't know how to shoot craps, but I did take part in the penny-pitching and in the pitch-'n'-putt games, gratefully pocketing a nickel or two and a few pennies when I won and cutting my losses to no more than a dime. It was from taking part in these impromptu games that I learned the "Who's Who" of National's members—judged not by their individual net worth or their private lives but by the weight of their bags and how much they tipped.

The going rate for eighteen holes was a dollar, and just about every one of the caddies contributed that earned dollar to the maintenance of the household in which they lived. The tip, on the other hand, usually was their own to keep, their "walking around" money. Thus the tip a golfer might give was of considerable importance. The customary tip was a quarter. There were tales of real sports who tipped fifty cents, but I never could verify them. I know that with one exception—one glorious, wonderful exception—no one ever tipped me more than a quarter. Bad luck was to caddy for a member who tipped only a dime. Also to be avoided if at all possible was another dime-tipper, the tip augmented by a stick of gum.

What all but the biggest and strongest of caddies hoped to avoid were the big leather trunklike bags in which some members wanted their clubs carried. Burdened with one of these heavyweights, by the twelfth hole a kid's carrying shoulder could be rubbed raw. Few, if any, bags in those days featured the generously padded straps seen on today's premier golf bags. Most often encountered were plain or thinly padded leather straps, the edges of which could bite. I was about fourteen when I first carried such a bag, and even though I tried to even things out by carrying it first on my right side then alternating the load to my left side, I still came home with raw and sore welts on both shoulders. My mother made me a stuffed pad out of an old sock, the idea being I could position it on my shoulder under my shirt. The pad (a) didn't work; it kept slipping. More important, it (b) earned hoots of derision from my caddy yard peers. I simply had to soldier on.

There was a bag caddies didn't mind carrying, although rarely was one used by the more skilled golfers. It was, simply, an off-white canvas tube, reinforced top and bottom and perhaps six inches in diameter. Its strap was either a narrow strip of the same off-white canvas or of brown leather. It was lightweight, less than sturdy, and unless carefully carried could prove itself to be maddeningly unbalanced. It was called a "Sunday bag," the implication being that its owner, not a serious golfer, was out for the exercise of a Sunday walk in the park and had opted to take along a few clubs for casual play. Such bags sold for a pittance, the price of $5 sticking in my mind. They often held the clubs of National's few lady golfers.

If you were lucky you got to make a loop with a halfway

decent golfer, someone who more often than not could keep the ball in play. If you were less than fortunate you spent a lot of time in the roughs and in the underbrush looking for balls that had been sliced or hooked, and you were expected to find them, period. If you couldn't find a mis-hit ball—if you didn't know exactly where it landed—the golfer for whom you were caddying wouldn't hesitate to let his or her displeasure be known. Overhearing yourself referred to as in some way incompetent reddened your ears and tended to diminish your enthusiasm for the job. On the other hand, finding a "lost" ball earned you no special praise and no assurance of a generous tip.

The tipping business at National always mystified me, as tipping does to this day. Its members were among the wealthiest men in the United States—tycoons, captains of industry, Social Register types, prominent judges, Wall Street brokers, corporate lawyers, political biggies, heirs of substantial fortunes—yet they could be downright stingy, even mean. A kid lugging his guts out on a dog day in August, hustling, doing the very best he could do was often viewed as little more than a mule. True, the kid may not have been the best caddy in the world, may not even have been able to find a mis-hit ball, but if he was really trying to please his employer didn't he rate more than a dime as a tip? What would a fifty-cent tip, even a dollar tip have meant to such men? Nothing. They were millionaires back when it counted, before there were rock stars and celebrity shortstops, yet most of them gave little or no thought to the beasts of burden carrying their bags.

Unlike most of the newer courses in this country, National was so laid out that playing No. 9 didn't bring you back to the clubhouse. Rather, the ninth green was the farthest point from the clubhouse. Off to the right of it, as you walked to the tenth tee, was a structure called, not surprisingly, the Halfway House. An attendant was always on duty, ready to dispense soft drinks, beer, candy bars, sandwiches, packs of chewing gum, and perhaps some fresh fruit, usually apples and maybe bananas. I think there might have been a water fountain there as well. It was the unexpressed hope of most caddies that they would be treated to a soft drink or a candy bar. Many of them were unable to bring something to eat from home. Others may have brought a sandwich but went out fairly late in the morning, and by the time they reached the ninth hole they were hungry. Yet too often no thought was given to the plight of such kids. Golfers would walk directly to the tenth tee, hit their drives, and continue playing. The really sad part of all this was that if a kid did bring a sandwich from home and was anticipating eating it when the round ended, he was apt to find that someone, also hungry, had beaten him to it. Swiping another kid's food was a no-no, yet it happened fairly regularly.

I can't recall a time when whomever I was caddying for failed to offer me a Halfway House soft drink or candy bar. I still can remember the treat of an ice-cold Coca-Cola running down my parched throat, or the taste of a Milky Way when I was so hungry I could have downed a moose. I suppose what caddies wanted subconsciously was the sugar that would fuel young bodies to hold up for the remaining nine holes.

In addition to carrying bags of clubs, caddies often were called upon to "shag balls." The assignment was given out when the professional was to give a lesson or when a golfer just wanted to hit balls. The elevated instructional/practice tee was located off to the right of and perhaps halfway up the eighteenth fairway. The bank in front of the tee slanted down to a macadamized road that led from National's main gate around past the beach-bordering bathhouse and up to the back of the golf shop and the caddy yard. Across the road was the actual practice range, consisting of a fairway and, at its far end, one or two sand bunkers around a casually maintained green and its pin, topped by a weary, faded flag. I say "casually maintained" because I never saw anyone actually putting on it, and the Old Man mentioned it only occasionally; its purpose was as a target for practice bunker shots.

A caddy summoned to shag balls was handed a canvas "shag bag" of perhaps fifty or more practice balls. The caddy would carry them—running, always running—to the practice tee, where at the direction of the professional or the practicing golfer he'd upend the bag, then, carrying the empty bag, he'd scamper down the bank, across the road, and out onto the fairway. How far out on the fairway he'd station himself would depend upon instructions shouted down from the practice tee, the distance determined by (a) the loft of the club being hit and (b) the ball-striking skill of the student or the golfer doing the hitting. The job then was to watch the flight of each hit ball, pick it up after it landed, and put it back in the bag. A bag thus filled was returned to the practice tee and the routine repeated. And repeated. And . . .

If the taker of a lesson was singularly unskilled, a ball-shagging caddy could find himself covering a lot of ground. Some balls would be dribbled down the bank in front of the tee, others would be slashed sharply right or left. A roundhouse hook might see a ball fly into the tall grass separating the edge of the fairway from the beach, making it difficult to find. Losing a ball on the practice range was a blow to one's self-esteem. Any such low point could be overcome, however, by successfully pulling off a stunt much admired by one's fellow caddies: catching an in-flight ball in the bag or catching it in the bag on one bounce. Here form was everything; you were supposed to bring it off looking like Joe DiMaggio going deep. A successful snag of an in-flight or one-bounce ball was a source of quiet pride. Bungling a catch was a source of sore knuckles.

The pay for this hour-long artistry or lack thereof was a uniform fifty cents. No tip.

• **14** •

All on a Golden Afternoon

ONE OF THE GREAT DAYS of my young life — of my life, period — began on a Sunday morning with my mother urging me to hurry and get ready for church. I didn't want to go to church, hated the whole idea of going to church; by that time I was beginning to suspect religion was, as Thomas Alva Edison so bluntly put it, "bunk." I don't know how or why I came to such a conclusion, only that religion and its strictures as dealt out by the Sunday school teachers and clerics of my youth was poison to a kid with even a smidgeon of imagination. I didn't know the Old Man's opinions on the subject, but I knew he wasn't a churchgoer.

On this particular morning I answered my mother's urgings with repeated cries of, "Gee, Mom, do I have to go?" and, "Mom, I don't want to go." Hearing all this, my father, his nose buried in the Sunday edition of the *New York Herald-Tribune*, suddenly lowered his newspaper and said in an even yet unmistakable tone, "If the kid doesn't want to go, he doesn't have to go."

And that was that. From that point on my churchgoing has been confined to prep school compulsory chapel, weddings, christenings, and funerals. Years later I learned why the Old Man had turned me loose.

In 1957 he and I toured through southern Scotland, including, of course, his hometown of St. Andrews. It was his first time there since, as a member of the AEF (American Expeditionary Force), he had stopped off to see his mother on his way home to the States at the end of World War I. While in St. Andrews he took me around to the no-longer-existent Tom Stewart works (makers of superb golf clubs once sold in this country by Spalding), where he had once been briefly employed. There he bought me a 3-, 5-, 7-, and 9-iron, a sand wedge, and two woods, a driver, and a spoon. He took me around to where he had gone to school, to where he had played soccer, to the shop of the green grocer to which he had once been apprenticed, around to the various sites for which "the auld gray toun" is now so well-known (for example, the cathedral ruins), even to the then-abandoned red brick gasworks down by the modest harbor in which a handful of fishing boats were moored or pulled up on a rocky beach.

But the pertinent place he took me — the place that on that epochal Sunday morning got me off the hook — was the church he had been forced to attend as a boy. After showing me the named pew in which his family sat, he told me how he hated the whole scene, how agonizing were the hours he was forced to sit while some dour minister of "the wee free kirk" (Scottish Presbyterianism) harangued the congregation about the evils of this or that, mostly the evils of pleasurable things. He said the only halfway enjoyable time he had spent in the church as a youngster was when on a certain Sunday a house fly, a comparative rarity in that part of the world, was flitting from parishioner to parishioner, from landing spot to landing spot, and his amused eyes followed the fly's every swoop and dart.

What being relieved of the need to attend church meant to me, apart from freedom, was that I was available to caddy. Weekends meant a proliferation of golfers, all of whom required caddies (I can't recall ever seeing a member of National carrying his own bag, not even a Sunday bag). At such times, now that I was available, I looked forward to making a loop. Accordingly, a peanut butter sandwich was prepared, wrapped, and stuffed in a pocket, maybe an apple would be placed in another pocket, and off I'd go, driven up near the golf shop by my father. By this time Joe Oakey, the caddymaster, knew me well enough to appreciate that barring being required to carry a trunk-of-a-bag I could finish all eighteen holes still on my feet, that I knew *how* to caddy, that I was a reasonably good ball hawk, that I didn't speak unless spoken to, and that I was polite. One Saturday morning, these qualifications presumably in mind, he wasn't reluctant to match me with a man named Patrick Andrew Valentine.

I didn't then and don't now know much about Mr. Valentine. I think he was from Chicago and may have been in some way related, possibly through marriage, to one of that city's meatpacking dynasties. I remember him as a fairly tall man in his mid-to-late forties, perhaps early fifties, who wore eyeglasses and sported a dark, neatly trimmed moustache. A couple of years after I first carried his bag, I read in a New York City tabloid that a ward of his had either done himself in or had tried to do himself in by jumping off a Manhattan building ledge. Apart from golf, what I really remember him for was that he owned and drove a 1937 kelly green Cord roadster with a light-tan canvas top, chromed flexible exterior exhaust pipes and all, and being a budding car nut, I thought that was the berries.

From observing and listening I had picked up a smattering of information as to how a golf course should be played. These days such knowledge might be referred to as "course management," and what it involves, really, is knowing where the ball should be hit and with what club to hit it. Scotland's famed and notoriously authoritarian professional caddies are said to be wizards at this sort of course management; after watching you swing once or twice they hand you the club they think is called for and tell you where to hit your shot. Only reluctantly—and scornfully—will they defer to your judgment should you happen to disagree. Although I knew nothing of that level of imperiousness, I did on occasion hand my man a club I thought he should use.

From the regular tee, the first hole at National is a 302-yard dogleg left par-4. All the holes at National are named, No. 1 being called Valley. As the name suggests, your tee shot is hit straight away (or if you're adventurous, slightly to the left) and down into a sort of bowl, leaving you with a lofted approach shot to an elevated green. The Saturday morning I first caddied for Patrick Andrew Valentine he hit a nice straight tee shot that came to rest just about at the bottom of the bowl, leaving him with perhaps a ninety-yard approach shot.

Caddies were trained to walk well in front of the player for whom they were caddying, the purpose being to get to the ball before the player did. Once there you were to take the bag off your shoulder and stand it upright within a couple of yards of the ball so that your employer could select a club with which to hit the next shot. When a club was selected you were to take several steps backward and stand absolutely still, making certain to not rattle the clubs in the bag. Failure to perform in such a manner, or any variation thereon, could earn you a mild rebuke from your employer, who later might well have a word with the caddymaster.

Following Patrick Andrew Valentine's serviceable drive I walked up to his ball, set the bag down, and drew halfway out of it his 7-iron, tipping its head in his direction. He studied the shot, looked at the proffered club, studied the shot again, and then asked, "Are you sure?" With the temerity and confidence only a fourteen-year-old can muster, I said yes, I was sure, pointing out that the green was elevated and that he had a slight breeze in his face. Whether uncertain or not I'll never know, but he took the 7-iron and hit his ball, which flew away in a graceful arc and out of sight. When we walked up to the green it was resting about ten feet from the pin. As he reached for the putter I was handing him he said, "That was the right club, caddy." He didn't make the putt but he did make par, and as we walked to the next tee I had the feeling my stock was bullish. He even asked my name.

He made par on No. 2 as well and was smiling broadly and exchanging easy banter with his playing partners as we walked to the next tee.

The third hole at National, a 441-yard par-4, calls for a tee shot hit off to the right, then an approach shot hit blind to an elevated, more or less saddle-shaped green. The hole is called Alps, and for good reason; the hill over which the second shot must be hit requires a precise and well-lofted shot if it's to be cleared. Hitting short of the green could be murder (in those days, anyway), requiring a third shot hit out of often terrible lies in tough, balky heather, a shot difficult to control. A golfer's best hope of making par on the hole is to be long and accurate off the tee so that the approach shot can be hit with a lofted iron. If you're short off the tee and are likely to need a wood to have any hope of getting home in two, you face a formidable challenge.

Patrick Andrew Valentine hit a pretty fair tee shot, straight but not terribly long. I thought his only hope for a decent second shot was his 5-wood, and that's the club I proffered him.

He seemed hesitant to take it, again asking me if I was sure. Hell, I was on a roll, so I said yes, that was the club he should hit. He did, and again found his ball resting on the green. And again he made par.

Up a steep bank behind the third green was (and still may be) a rather large brass bell, the sounding of which signaled golfers waiting on the fairway below that the green was clear. When my man's second putt dropped for par and he and the men he was playing with (along with their caddies) headed for the tee on No. 4, I all but floated up to the bell and with new-found authority decisively yanked its clapper.

That memorable Saturday my man shot 76, three over par, according to him the very best golf he'd ever played in his entire life. To say he was delighted is to understate it by half. The congratulations of his playing partners were gratefully and graciously received, and even I found myself grinning widely. When we walked off the eighteenth green he asked if I would be available the following day, say about nine o'clock. I said I would be, and having learned my full name, that I was the greenkeeper's son, and where I lived, he said, "I'll come by about eight o'clock and pick you up." All that was fine, but I noticed he wasn't reaching in his pocket in a gesture that suggested he was about to pay me. Instead he said he'd pay me at the completion of our round the following day. I turned his bag in at the golf shop and walked home, uncertain and a little uneasy, wondering if I really was going to be paid.

Prior to that next morning I knew very little about a Cord.

I'd seen pictures of the car in newspaper and magazine advertisements but couldn't recall ever seeing one in the flesh, although I'm fairly certain more than one Southampton summer sport owned such a car. Imagine, then, my wonder and delight when this sleek, bright-green beauty pulled into the cottage yard and sounded its horn. I gave my mother a hasty kiss and dashed out the kitchen lobby door, anxious to climb in and have a look around. He opened the passenger-side door for me and bade me get in, saying, "Good morning, Billy. Ready to go to work?" I'm sure I answered appropriately, but I suddenly was drunk on the car, especially its burnished aluminum dashboard and its display of serious instruments. Other than the dashboard and the car's exterior, I draw a blank, even that first ride to the clubhouse beyond recall.

Patrick Andrew Valentine shot 82 that Sunday, and when we came off the eighteenth green he expressed his thanks and handed me a $5 bill. I've been miserable with math all my life but even then I knew $5 represented $2.50 per round, an unheard of sum for a caddy to be paid in those days, even big, strong, experienced caddies. That a fourteen-year-old kid with sore shoulders was paid $2.50 for eighteen holes was nothing short of miraculous. Again I walked home, this time full of joy, my feet hardly touching the ground.

Throughout the summer I caddied for him a couple of additional times, always on a Saturday and the following Sunday. He'd call the house on a preceding Thursday or Friday to ask if I was available, and he always came by in the Cord to pick me up. I was paid with a $5 bill each Sunday afternoon. Given such a sum, it's no wonder the man and his Cord have been stuck in my mind ever since.

I don't recall what I did with the money—probably spent part of it on yet another pair of the camp moccasins in which, along with tennis sneakers, I lived. In any event, having an unencumbered and unspoken-for $5 bill burning the proverbial hole in my pocket gave me my first awareness of capitalism.

All the Jolly Fellows

STAID BEHAVIOR WASN'T ALWAYS the operative word at National. Given its venerability, its impressive links-type course, its manorial clubhouse overlooking Great Peconic Bay, its more or less Social Register membership, and its exalted stature in the history of American golf, it's hard to imagine it as ever being the scene of off-the-wall behavior. Yet among the members were a number of what I suppose might be referred to as eccentrics.

There was, for example, a man who at times when in his cups liked to crunch up soda crackers and scatter them down the stairs to the founders locker room, where a patient and understanding attendant named Arthur Ayers swept them up to the accompaniment of the man's derisive laughter.

And there was another over-served sport who once climbed into his Pierce-Arrow determined to drive the length of the golf course. Why was never made clear, but his enthusiasm for the scheme waned about halfway down the fifth fairway, at which point he pulled off into some bordering rough and dozed off. Fortunately, he hadn't driven on any of the greens.

There was a rather full former boxing champion who was reported to have once climbed naked out of his dormer room and onto the clubhouse roof. And there was the perennial first-round leader of the club's annual thirty-six-hole championship, who was given to celebrating his good fortune to such an extent that for the next day's second round he was hard-pressed to even find the course, let alone play it.

There was, too, a very well-known business executive—virtually a celebrity, in fact—who wobbled out of the club bar late one Saturday afternoon and despite what I'm sure was a gallant effort to avoid doing so nonetheless crashed his gorgeous right-hand-drive English Lagonda automobile into one of the stone pillars of the entrance gate.

The proverbial cake, however, may have been taken by a man who during the summer months occasionally enjoyed watching caddies dive for golf balls he'd hit into the bay down behind the first tee. At such times he was carrying a load, of course, but that didn't make his behavior any less odd. He'd come rolling into the shop, ask that his driver be fetched from the bag room, then buy a dozen new top-of-the-line Dunlop balls—always Dunlops—and a box of Reddy tees. Purchases and driver in hand, he'd tack out of the shop and up the nearby wooden steps to the plateau of the first tee, all the while chuckling to himself, presumably in anticipation of the fun he was about to have.

The presence of any potential employer on the first tee was noted as if by radar by the caddies awaiting assignment, and once our man appeared all of them knew what to expect. From the back edge of the tee the man would call out in the direction of the shed, "Any of you kids want to go swimming?" The day usually being hot and there being no better prospect at hand, some of the caddies would scramble down the road to the nearby beach below, toss off their shirts and pants, shoes and socks, and in their underwear or in the buff dive into the water. They swam or waded out to a point at which they could barely touch bottom, then they turned and faced the man on the tee awaiting their deployment.

Depending upon the heft of the load he was carrying, he'd either tee a ball up himself or, had he been really over-served, ask that a caddy be summoned to assist him. Once a ball — a brand-new seventy-five-cent ball, mind you, this at the tail end of the Depression — was teed up, he'd make a surprisingly graceful and sober swing and knock it out into the bay. Then, grinning, laughing, he'd watch as the swimming caddies thrashed the water and dove bottoms-up to determine which one would come up with the ball. When the ball was retrieved and raised aloft or, in some instances, given up for lost, the process would be repeated, each time giving the man what appeared to be gratifying amusement.

When the dozen new balls were exhausted, he'd drop his club on the tee or, if assistance had been necessary, hand it to the caddy along with a dollar bill. He would then wobble off in the direction of the clubhouse, there presumably to seek further sustenance.

Apart from never knowing the man to play a round of golf, what to my young mind made his performance truly bizarre was that he never removed the cellophane wrapper in which each new Dunlop ball was sealed; he'd whack 'em out into the bay wrapper and all. I later was told most of the caddies who retrieved the new balls sold them for thirty-five or fifty cents each at what then was Southampton's only public golf course.

Strong drink also played a key role in another indelible memory. It remains indelible because as a result of the incident the Old Man very nearly blew a gasket.

It seems that on a summer Saturday night — this may have been 1939 or 1940 — a carnival was playing on a lot at what then was the outskirts of town. Well-fueled, a foursome of jolly fellows, at least two of them members of National, rolled into the carnival; there they became captivated by its calliope. So captivated were they, they decided it would serve as ideal accompaniment for the round the four of them planned to play the following morning. Accordingly, they hired the calliope, its operator, and the driver of the flatbed truck upon which it sat to show up at the first tee the next morning at a certain hour, at which time its garish music would accompany them as they played the famed old course's hallowed holes.

Whatever sleep they may or may not have had overnight apparently did nothing to deter them from this scheme, all four appearing on the first tee at the appointed hour, reportedly looking somewhat worn. Right on cue the calliope and its crew arrived, and despite suggestions from a few other members that perhaps the entire venture should be called off, the foursome waved the maestro into action, teed up, hit their drives, and started down the path leading off the first tee. The calliope was banging out "Entrance of the Gladiators" (or some tune very much like it) as its truck eased down a dirt road paralleling the fairway.

Since the greenkeeper's cottage was nearby and even though Sunday presumably was his day off, my father was advised of what was afoot and was asked what should be done about it. Keep in mind that in those days at clubs such as National, democracy—égalité—was not a strong suit. The staff was the staff, period, and as such it was expected to tip its collective hat (figuratively and sometimes even literally) to the club's wealthy membership. The Old Man, then, was in no position to order that the calliope be silenced and removed from the premises.

Nonetheless, my absolutely furious father piled into his pickup truck and drove on the golf course roads toward the clubhouse, where he encountered, wending its way up the dirt road at the side of the second fairway, the calliope. He pulled off to one side, got out, and presumably forced a smile and nodded in the direction of the merrymakers as they trudged up the second fairway. He then turned to the slowly passing truck and stepped up on the driver-side running board.

I never was told what was said, but after going another

twenty yards or so both the flatbed and the music came to a halt. The driver climbed down, walked over in the direction of the foursome, and explained that the calliope had broken down and that he'd have to take it back to the lot to repair it in time for the carnival's afternoon opening. The foursome, in all likelihood by then finding the gag as well as their jocularity wearing thin, seemed not to mind. They thanked him and went on their way.

The last seen of the flatbed truck and its monstrous calliope, its gaudy red paint much likely equaled only by the assured choleric red of my father's face, it was passing through National's stately gates.

• **16** •

Having a Ball

ANYONE MINDFUL OF THE FRENZIED merchandising that has plagued—yes, plagued—golf over the past three or so decades has to be both amused and appalled. The clubs with which today's game is played have been hawked like snake oil from the back of a wagon—a cure-all in every bottle, step right up. It's to laugh.

Qualities just short of miraculous, perhaps even divinity, have been claimed for golf balls in their manufacturers' mad scramble to snag and hold the attention of the gullible. You can have a slice swing worse than a cane cutter wielding a machete, goes the implication, and this or that ball will fly straight and far every time. Sure.

The appeals to credulity go on—golf shoes that "grip the ground," logoed golf shirts that "keep you dry and comfortable, even on the hottest days," jackets that allow "a free and easy swing," golf socks that promise not only luxury but all-day comfort, couturier-designed women's golf apparel, complete with ever-so-cute accessories.

I'm no exception. Joe Gullible here. I've gone through drivers and putters as if they were paper towels. Even at my age I find myself receptive to pitches that assure me I can hit a ball 220 yards off a tee, pitches that promise to cure my putting yips. The beautiful real wood woods handmade by Joe Oakey over seventy years ago sold for about $30; today's assembly line wonder rods sell for upwards of $500 or more.

The whole thing is out of whack, the basic truth being that regardless of club and ball technology, and regardless of what is paid for the products of such technology, "It don't mean a thing if you ain't got that swing."

The premier golf ball at National in the late 1930s was the Penfold 75, the "75" reflecting its retail price. Not only was it the bestseller in Alick Gerard's golf shop, it was deemed—mysteriously, of course—to "go farther" than other balls. Also available and a pretty good seller was the Penfold 35, again the number being its price. During one summer when I clerked now and then in the shop (before heading off for a stint as a junior counselor at a 4-H camp), I often wondered why men of what I assumed was great wealth would opt for the thirty-five-cent ball. Just about all those who bought the cheaper ball weren't very good golfers, and now that I think of it again I suppose the theory was akin to "Why throw good money after bad?"

Also in the thirty-five-cent end of the ball business was one manufactured by Acushnet, whose premium ball then (and now, in all its renderings) was the Titleist. I recall that Dunlop offered a thirty-five-center (or perhaps a fifty-center) as well, but it didn't sell on a par with the cheaper Penfolds and Achusnets.

In addition to the Titleist, close behind the Penfold 75 in consumer appeal was the Spalding Dot. There also was a softer ball called the Spalding Dash, which didn't sell nearly as well as the Dot. The cover of the Dash may have featured a square mesh pattern common to many golf balls throughout the 1920s and '30s, but its days were numbered once manufacturers and their advertising agencies discovered wind tunnels and aerodynamics; their ads could assure consumers that the mesh pattern's squares lacked the superior aerodynamic flight characteristics of the dimpled ball. Both Spaldings sold for seventy-five cents.

Other balls also selling for seventy-five cents each were the Wilson K28, the Silver King, the North British, the Dunlop 75, and the U.S. Royal Blue. I can't swear to this, but I'm reasonably certain more than one of the offerings available in the shop were house label balls — that is, balls made to a brand name's specifications by a common manufacturer, at the time very likely by the Worthington Golf Ball Company of Elyria, Ohio.

All of the top-name balls had natural balata covers. My desktop dictionary defines balata as "a substance like gutta-percha that is the dried juice of tropical American trees of the sapodilla family and is used especially in belting and golf balls." Whatever. All I know is that the stuff cut easily. If you hawked balls, about half of those you picked up favored you with a big permanent smile, a sure sign of a mis-hit shot with an iron, the comparatively sharp leading edge of the club's sole having cut through the balata like the proverbial hot knife through butter. Such balls were useless for golf, of course, but they had great appeal for boys seeking answers to the great mysteries of life.

Assuming a wide enough "smile" in such a ball (especially one that had been burned in a grass or brush fire), a penknife and a bit of determination could peel away the rest of the cover, exposing a small sphere of continuous, tightly wound rubber thread. Like a kitten toying with a ball of knitting wool, a kid fiddling with the rubber thread of a wound ball could find delight in unwinding it, first locating the end of the thread, then holding the end in one hand and throwing the ball into the air as hard and as far as he could. Or, the end of the thread in hand, he could use a hand-over-hand motion and simply unwind it, in the process building up at his feet a gratifying mound of rubber thread. However the rubber thread was unwound, the treasure was to be found at the ball's core.

When the first wound balls (wound with rubber thread) came on the market in the early 1900s, just about every substance imaginable was experimented with for the core — soap, mercury, loose steel balls, castor oil, glycerin, blood, compressed air, pulverized metal, cork, rubber, human hair (I'm not making this up; see Gary Wiren's *PGA Manual of Golf*, page 13). At the time of which I'm writing all this research boiled down to two cores: one a solid sphere of pink or pale-green rubber, the other a malleable rubber sack of highly viscous and mysterious liquid, its consistency not unlike that of toothpaste. Such a core was a prize, principally because it provided an element of always-appealing danger.

Caddy shed scuttlebutt had it that the stuff in the little rubber sack was "acid." What kind of acid no one knew, only that if you got any on your person you'd be burned, perhaps even have the tip of a finger eaten away. Fearsome stuff, then, best avoided. But as it so often does with boys, curiosity conquered fear; gingerly, the sack would be sliced open, its contents squeezed out and at first carefully sniffed. Then the hero within would step forward, assured there could be no harm in just touching the stuff. Besides, it could immediately be wiped off, right? And so, tenuously, the tip of a finger would be extended and the mystery liquid touched.

Nothing happened. Absolutely nothing. For all intents and purposes the stuff was as harmless as Vaseline, and to this day I have no idea what it was — some form of glycerin, I suspect. Anyway, once fear had been conquered and the rubber sack of stuff rewardingly squeezed out and emptied, the daring experiment was replaced by enthusiasm for the little ball of solid rubber to be found at the core of most wound golf balls. It was extremely lively, bounded high when bounced, and, if swatted like a baseball with a stick or a length of shingle lath, could fly extremely rewarding distances. Thus it required little imagination to be Joe DiMaggio belting one out of the park.

There was, however, one brand of golf ball that remained a mystery, mainly because at the time I never came across one. And as Damon Runyan titled one of his short stories, "There's a Story Goes with It."

The 1939 British Open was played on the Old Course at St. Andrews and was won by a Brit named Richard Burton with a seventy-two-hole score of 290. Finishing two strokes back in second place was an American named Johnny Bulla, who carried on his strong back the hopes of all his countrymen and not just those of U.S. golfers.

At the time, the British Open (or as the Brits refer to it, "The Open") had last been won by an American—Denny Shute—in 1933. More to the point was that Bulla was playing the event with a thirty-five-cent ball marketed by an American drugstore chain, and in splashy pretournament newspaper ads the drugstore chain made sure everyone coast to coast was aware of it. Profit to a retailer on the sale of a premium seventy-five-cent ball may have been as much as twenty-five or thirty-five cents; Bulla winning "The Open" with a thirty-five-cent ball would have created a financial panic in golf shops worldwide. You can appreciate, then, how anxiously news of the tournament was received.

Newspapers did a good job of day-after coverage, but what was crucial, with Bulla and his thirty-five-cent ball very much in the hunt, was live news of the final round, news obtainable only on radio in an overseas shortwave broadcast by the BBC (British Broadcasting Corporation). If Bulla won on Sunday it would be Blue Monday in the world's golf shops, certainly in National's golf shop. I don't recall whether or not a radio was standard equipment in the shop, but on the Sunday of the tournament's final round a small radio occupied a prominent spot on a table behind the glass-fronted case in which golf balls, tees, half-gloves (made of buttery-soft leather that smelled delicious), a couple of rain jackets, and three or four woolen sweaters were displayed. Seated right and left of the radio and hovering over its one speaker were two fiftyish Scotsmen—my father and Alick Gerard, both wearing a serious expression.

In these days of clear-as-a-bell television and radio transmissions, it may be difficult for most people to appreciate just how finicky radio reception could be seventy years ago, especially reception of a broadcast from overseas. Squeaks, squawks, and whistles were common, eruptions of static simply a given. The hope was that occasionally filtering through all the noise would be discernible information—in the instance of National's golf shop and the 1939 British Open, information of who was winning.

"It'll no do if Bulla wins," said Alick Gerard, an even more serious expression on his florid face.

"Be a bloody disaster," agreed my father.

"First steel shafts, and now a bloody thirty-five-cent ball," said Alick Gerard.

"A damn shame," said my father.

But finally through the static and the squeaks and the squawks came the report that Burton had won, and once again serenity returned to the golf shop at National.

Bulla, whose knockaround pal was Sam Snead, continued as a marquee player until well after World War II, but the thirty-five-cent ball he touted—called a PoDo—pretty much faded from consciousness, seen only now and then on public golf courses. I remember once really tagging a drive while in college and having one of the guys in my foursome kid me by saying I must be playing a "needled" PoDo.

The Way It Was, Part II

IN THESE DAYS of the dazzling Tiger Woods and his con-
temporaries, just about all of whom can be seen on television any weekend year-round and whose exploits are featured
in newspapers and magazines worldwide, it may be hard to
believe there was a time when play-for-pay golfers toiled in
comparative anonymity. The big golf noise insofar as media
extant in the 1930s were concerned (newspapers, magazines,
radio stations, and newsreels, or simply "the press") was
amateur golf. While many nongolfers may have been able
to recognize the name Bobby Jones, few could identify, say,
Bobby Cruickshank or Ralph Guldahl (winner of the 1937 and
1938 U.S. Open). If you mentioned the name Picard, chances
were it might be identified as that of a well-known physicist
(Auguste Piccard, father of oceanographer Jacques Piccard).
Yet Henry Picard was the 1939 winner of the PGA Championship. In truth, during the '30s you would have to have been a

die-hard devotee of the sports pages to recognize and properly place Ky Lafoon, Olin Dutra, Ed Dudley, or Johnny Revolta.

As for women professional golfers, they were virtually unknown. For most of the decade the woman golfer with whom Mr. and Mrs. John Q. Public might be familiar was six-time U.S. Women's Amateur Champion Glenna Collett Vare, a holdover from the 1920s. Babe Didrikson (later Babe Zaharias), a powerhouse from Texas who dominated women's track and field events during the 1932 Olympics in Los Angeles, was known to play good golf (but she was equally well-known, perhaps more so, for a stunt during spring training one year when she pitched a few innings for the then Brooklyn Dodgers). It wasn't until the incomparable Patty Berg turned pro in 1940 and began barnstorming the nation staging clinics and playing exhibition matches that most people even knew there was such a thing as women's professional golf.

That in mind, it may be opportune to differentiate between a golf professional and a professional golfer. How people tend to confuse the two can be illustrated by a golf pro I know who while pumping gasoline one day at a self-serve somehow fell into conversation with a fellow pumper. Improbably, they got to talking about what they did for a living, and when my friend identified himself as a golf pro, the fellow pumper, a furniture salesman, said, "Yeah? You ever play in the U.S. Open?" When my friend said he hadn't the other guy lost interest in further conversation.

A professional golfer is someone who plays golf for a living, that is, he or she tries to qualify for and enter tournaments and similar events that pay prize money. The more successful he or she is—the more consistent he or she is in posting low scores—the more money the professional golfer earns. Many such golfers, both men and women, play or played on the major professional tours and have become multimillionaires. Most, however, are golfing nomads who toil in virtual anonymity on so-called mini tours—localized tournaments for which the prize money is comparatively meager. A comment often heard among the entrants in such events, many of whom operate out of the backs of minivans and subsist on diets of fast food, is, "One of these days I'm going to have to get a real job."

The golf professional is someone who serves golf in much the same way any professional serves his or her clientele. He or she teaches golf, interprets its rules, deals in its playing equipment and in its accompanying accessories, sets up and oversees various golfing events, analyzes and attempts to correct swing faults, and in general provides a shoulder upon which the golfers under his or her cognizance can weep, seek solace, gnash teeth, or exult in the running down of a thirty-five-foot putt.

Golfers on the PGA Tour, the LPGA Tour, the PGA Champions (that is, Senior) Tour, and the like occupy a sort of golfing Valhalla; to paraphrase a comment Bobby Jones once made regarding Jack Nicklaus, they play a game with which most golfers are not now and never will be familiar. The typical golf professional, on the other hand, lives in a world of gripes, slices, hooks, foozled irons, yipped putts, "fried egg" sand shots, high-risk merchandise inventories, wounded feelings, and misinterpreted rules. The gods of golf order Chateau Lafite Rothschild and filet mignon, while mere golf professionals tend to pop a can of beer and ask, "What's for supper?"

In the immediate days leading up to America's entry into World War II, professional golf's Big Three—Byron Nelson, Ben Hogan, and Sam Snead—made an unprecedented impression on the public consciousness. You'd have to have been living in a cave to not have read in your newspaper's sports pages or seen and heard in a newsreel that as a kid West Virginia hillbilly Sam Snead played golf in his bare feet, or that Texan Ben Hogan brought to the game a sort of deadly earnestness, a degree of concentration that made him seem cold and remote. You might even have read that as a struggling play-for-pay pro, Byron Nelson (also a Texan), before overhauling his swing in order to hit the ball straight, went through drivers—or his hand-hewn versions of drivers, anyway—as one would go through conical paper drinking cups.

But before these worthies began to capture the public's attention, the immortal Bobby Jones and perhaps Walter Hagen and Gene Sarazen excepted, golf news in this country tended to center around amateurs with names such as Jess Sweetser, George Dunlap Jr., Lawson Little (later a touring pro), Max Marston, Johnny Goodman (winner of the 1933 U.S. Open as an amateur), Willie Turnesa, Ray Billows, Marvin "Bud"

Ward, Skee Riegel, Charles Kocsis, T. Suffren "Tommy" Tailer, Charles Yates, Frank Strafaci, Dick Chapman, Tony Manero, and a host of others who, depending upon where you lived and what newspaper you read, dominated whatever golf news there was to be found in Monday editions. The weekend exploits of, say, Chuck Kocsis, who lived and played most of his golf in the Detroit area, were very apt to shove below the fold a paper's sports-pages accounts of a far-off Los Angeles Open.

Keep in mind, too, that the events in which these heroes played were match play, mano-a-mano contests that brought into play psychology as much as they did skill. To this day my preference is match play rather than medal, or stroke play. To me a golf match is what the game's all about. Although the first two rounds of the U.S. Amateur are at stroke play, even now the last six rounds are at match play, and I would bet not three golfers in ten can name the reigning champion.

At National one year there was an exhibition by New York metropolitan area amateur star Ellis Knowles, and on another occasion an exhibition by Eugene V. Homans, runner-up to Bobby Jones in the U.S. Amateur of 1930, the year the latter also won the U.S. Open and the British Amateur as well as the British Open, thus completing golf's "Grand Slam." The galleries that followed these exhibitions at National numbered perhaps fifty or so, all but a few of whom were club members or guests of club members. Any auslanders present were apt to be famed sportswriter Grantland Rice or the golf writer from the *New York Herald-Tribune*. Decorum and silence were the order of the day, each superb shot greeted by subdued exclamations of appreciation and polite applause . . . and with not a candy wrapper, a Port-a-Let, or a hotdog vendor in sight.

During the 1930s such exhibitions were common at golf and country clubs throughout the United States. For example, after gaining a name for herself as the winner of the 1934 Minneapolis Women's City Championship at the age of sixteen, Patty Berg often spent Sundays playing exhibitions at venues throughout the upper Midwest. Usually she played with the local pro or with the local men's club champion. Hundreds of fans followed these exhibitions, fans who on the following day could read about it in their local newspaper.

In contrast, on a fine day in the late 1980s, when Greg Norman was playing the most exciting golf of his career, he took part in a local fund-raising tournament at a course in southwest Florida and drew a gallery numbering all of forty-four. If recent galleries are any indication, people presumably still will turn out to follow icon Arnold Palmer even if he's in a wheelchair and requires a pulmotor and a nurse in attendance at all times, but only Tiger Woods is apt to draw galleries even close in number to those who in pretelevision days turned out to follow Jones, or Chick Evans, or even Walter Travis.

My first brush with golfing glory was as a caddy for a man named Finlay S. Douglas. You'd have to be a student of golf to recognize his name and know his role in the game's history in this country. Originally from St. Andrews, Douglas won the fourth-ever U.S. Amateur in 1898 at the age of twenty-three.

For the next several years he was a dogged contender to repeat as champion, his great rival being Walter Travis, with whom he often played exhibition matches. One of his frequent opponents during this period was National's founder, Charles Blair Macdonald, so it's not to be wondered at that Douglas was one of the club's original founders. Known at the turn of the century as one of the game's longest hitters, he went on to become president of the USGA (1929–30). His name was mentioned often in our house, in part because of his position in golf but more often because he was a St. Andrews man.

Previously I mentioned my father granting me a reprieve from the oppression of attending church, his magnanimity stemming not so much from his agnosticism as from his memory of spending forced, endless, and agonizing hours trapped in the strictures of Victorian Presbyterianism. According to him, the only pleasure he ever got from religious instruction was as a Sunday school youngster, his teacher a young man named Finlay S. Douglas.

It may have been this connection more than any other reason that on one hot summer Saturday I got the assignment to caddy for Douglas. I was a neophyte caddy at the time and couldn't have been more than fourteen. Even so I remember receiving a most friendly, even genial greeting from my employer; he knew who I was and I certainly knew who he was, and I was determined to do a good job of caddying for him. I can't remember a single thing about making that loop, but I know I came away from the experience feeling I had been in the presence of history, and ever since it has been a real zing for me to tell golf buffs that I once caddied for Finlay S. Douglas.

On another occasion I caddied in a foursome that included Juan T. Trippe, founder and president of Pan-American Airways. Trippe maintained a summer home in the Hamptons but now and then arrived at National in a seaplane that landed on Great Peconic Bay and taxied to the beach near the club's bathhouse. His arrivals and departures in the black-and-orange seaplane (a Sikorsky s-38, perhaps) were dramatic stuff and the subject of much chatter among the caddies, some of whom wondered aloud what it would be like to be rich enough to have your own seaplane. The speculation was that Trippe probably had lunch in his New York skyscraper office, then decided to summon his pilot and zip out to National for a fast nine holes, bringing with him a playing partner or two.

Whether flown out in the seaplane or not, one of Trippe's playing partners in the foursome in which I caddied was Jess Sweetser, a Yale man who won the U.S. Amateur in 1922 and, despite a severe case of the flu, the British Amateur in 1926. Bobby Jones being the exception, Sweetser probably was the premier American amateur throughout the 1920s. I knew who he was and was appropriately impressed by the gravity of my having been retained to caddy in the foursome.

Trippe was a waggler, a repetitive waggler, an endless waggler, a numbing waggler. He'd address his shot, waggle, waggle some more, then waggle even more, and he would continue waggling as the seconds ticked by, seemingly unwilling or unable to pull the trigger. He wasn't a bad golfer, as I recall, just a singularly reluctant one . . . or so it seemed.

You can imagine how this endless dithering went down with Sweetser. I still can picture him on National's first tee, expecting Trippe to let fly at any moment but soon becoming aware that nothing was happening. Nothing—just more waggles. Finally, exasperated, he barked, "For crissake, Trippe, hit the goddamn ball!"

The shock of someone, even Jess Sweetser, speaking to a captain of American industry in such a manner made the incident indelible on my mind. Years later I played in a Connecticut golf outing at which I got to chat with Sweetser, and I mentioned the incident, including reminding him of what he had said.

"I said that?" he asked, smiling. "Yeah, I must have. I probably said that to Trippe so often he was used to it."

· 18 ·

Landmarks

DOWN THROUGH THE YEARS various writers on the subjects of golf courses and golf course architecture have been generous in their praise of National, with good reason; it really is a superb layout, and playing it is a pleasure. According to no less an authority than famed golf course architect Robert Trent Jones, the building of National "sowed the seed of modern golf course design." Charles Blair Macdonald took what he deemed to be the best features of the better British courses and adapted them to the site upon which National is built. Thus the individual holes bear the names of those from which they were adapted, none exact duplicates yet all executed in the spirit of their originals, some of them most memorable.

No. 7, for example, a 462-yard par-5 (from the regular tee), was named St. Andrews, quite possibly for the deep and steeply walled pot bunker that guarded the green, a bunker reminiscent of the monster that lurks by the green of the Road

Hole on the Old Course. The version at National was smaller but not much kinder. In fact, there was a sort of stepladder golfers had to use to enter and exit it. I once caddied in a foursome and stood by in burning embarrassment as an absolutely furious and berserk banker named Charles Mitchell took seven strokes to extricate his ball from its bruising clutch.

No. 14, as mentioned earlier a 336-yard par-4, was named Cape. I don't know the location of the hole upon which it was patterned, but Robert Trent Jones termed Macdonald's version "a truly splendid golf hole." A dogleg right, the drive had to be hit over water, ideally straightaway to the top of a small hill. Assuming a decent drive, the key to par or better was the approach shot, which had to be hit to a green guarded on the right by both a small pond and a sort of waste bunker, on the left by sand and scrub growth, in back by a huge semicircular bunker, and a bit farther on another pond. The hole's beauty, the views it afforded (for example, Bull's Head Bay off to the right), and the comparatively short shot required to reach home could lull a golfer into underestimating its potential for disaster. Not only did the shot have to be directionally accurate, it had to be of just the right length, preferably landing on the front part of the green. Hit it a little too loud and you could wind up in the back bunker. Hit it really loud and you were wet.

On one occasion I caddied for a man named Roger Tuckerman, who—in addition to affecting a hunched-over, elbows-out-like-wings putting style similar to that of veteran

Deemed "a truly splendid golf hole" by famed golf course architect
Robert Trent Jones, No. 14 at National is the hole upon which a
man I was caddying for met self-imposed disaster. The pond
(*upper left*) is the one in which I was the semi-frozen and
reluctant searcher for a club that had slipped out of a
golfer's hands. (Courtesy of Marvin E. Newman.)

professional golfer Leo Diegel—had an awkward swing that betrayed him at the most inopportune times. One such time was when, his short drive on No. 14 safely landed in the fairway, he sliced his second shot—a 5-wood—into the right-side pond. He dropped another ball and slashed at it, knocking it left and into a bunker. All but choking in rage and embarrassment (although I was the only witness as he was playing alone), he dropped a third ball and this time, *really* overcorrecting, hooked it far to the left of the green and into some scrub bushes. And with that he stormed off to the tee on No. 15. Had I known anything about cardiac arrest I would have had cause to worry. On the other hand, he was the guy who tipped a dime and a stick of gum.

National's most memorable hole to me was and still is No. 16. It was an uphill slight dogleg right, the distance from the regular tee listed on the card as 381 yards, a par-4. It was called Punchbowl for the very good reason that the green was just that, a bowl-shaped depression steeply banked on all sides. Apart from the unusual green, what gave the hole its zest were two large and deep hollows about halfway out, the left-side one in short grass, the right-side one in Purgatory, its calf-length rough all but impossible to escape. Grown men who pulled or hooked a drive into the bowl on the left were known to whimper, those who sliced into the bowl on the right to weep. A party that successfully negotiated No. 16 had light hearts as they climbed up out of the green's bowl and advanced to the seventeenth tee.

Another memory is of the shingled windmill on a rise between the second fairway and the sixteenth green, over which it and its stationary sails loomed. Back then it was (and I think still is) the most prominent thing on the horizon, and my curiosity about it was more than piqued. Of course I was forbidden to enter it and of course I couldn't wait to see what was inside. I gained entry through one of its windows and found a lot of heavy overhead wooden beams and braces, the purposes of which I didn't understand, and on the floor what I took to be parts and gears of some sort of pump, the lot of it covered in dust. It was kind of scary, too; gusts of wind would cause the windmill's sails to creak ominously, a sound that with only a thin slice of childhood imagination suggested—what? Ghosts? There was a ladder leading to an upper platform, and obviously that had to be climbed and the platform explored. From the platform I could see the chocks that prevented the windmill's four sails from rotating.

A few years ago, thanks to its then greenkeeper, my wife and I were able to play the wonderful old course, and one of the first things my eyes went to was the windmill. It's as much a part of National as is the lobster salad.

In addition to a then rarely used bathhouse, National afforded its members and their guests a yacht basin at which fairly large boats could be tied up. A boat would come in off Great Peconic Bay, tie up, and be met by the club's station wagon, which in turn would ferry the occupants of the boat up to the nearby clubhouse. Following a round of golf, or perhaps

Situated on National's highest elevation, between No. 2 and
No. 16, its windmill may once have pumped irrigation water
but for decades has served only as a distinctive landmark.
Note the serious rough. (Photo courtesy of the author.)

just lunch, the station wagon would return them to the yacht
basin and the boat would depart. I suppose that sort of indul-
gence takes place somewhere in the world these days, but it
seemed to me then (as it does now) the epitome of the privi-
leges attendant upon wealth.

Entry to the basin was through a narrow channel in which
the water of incoming and outgoing tides raced at a brisk clip.
If a fairly large boat entered the channel when the incoming

tide was really pouring it on, the boat was apt to rocket toward the basin's pilings, causing its helmsman a momentary flash of panic. On duty for such arrivals was the basin's overseer, a gentle man named Bill Grey. He and his wife and two college-age daughters lived in a small cottage that was the basin's most prominent feature.

Fuel was available, as were certain yachting basics—rope, fenders, life preservers, lightweight anchors, and so on, all of which would be furnished upon request and charged to a member's account. If food and drink provisions were needed, a list was handed to "Captain" Grey, who in turn would pass it to the driver of the club's station wagon, who in turn would drive into Southampton and buy whatever was on the list.

If a boat were to come through the channel and bear around to the left for several hundred yards, it would come to a fork, the water on the right leading to Bull's Head Bay, the water on the left to a remote retreat owned by a man named H. H. Rogers. The retreat was called "The Port of Missing Men," its most notable feature, apart from its size, a cavernous under-the-house area in which a fairly good-sized boat could be docked. My reading of F. Scott Fitzgerald's *The Great Gatsby* was some years in the future, but even back then—being a child of Prohibition—I could imagine cases of bootleg scotch being offloaded from a yacht anchored in the bay and later poured for the sustenance of Rogers's "missing men" guests.

National's membership at the time included men who owned truly impressive yachts, yachts too large to enter the basin and tie up. These would anchor out in the bay, their owners and guests ferried to and fro in a Chris-Craft or similar powerboat lowered from the yacht's deck.

A man named L. Gordon Hamersley owned a black two-masted schooner named *Countess*, and because he owned a big white house on the edge of nearby Bull's Head Bay, *Countess* was a frequent visitor. I was very impressed by it because (a) it was sleek and (b) I'd been told it regularly took part in the annual offshore Marblehead (Massachusetts) Race. In sailboating circles in those days the race was big news, and I read about it in the *Herald-Tribune*.

Even bigger was *Migrant*, owned by a man named Carll Tucker. It was a three-masted schooner, also painted black and one of the most impressive private yachts I've ever seen. Not only did its size make an impression on me, but it was my understanding the live-aboard crew numbered almost thirty. When I was younger my mother's father had read to me Richard Henry Dana Jr.'s *Two Years Before the Mast*, and no special imagination was needed to picture myself scampering up *Migrant*'s rigging as it plowed through aquamarine Caribbean waters, the legs of my sailor's white ducks flapping in the wind. I remember sailing my modest and somewhat porous catboat out to take a close look at and photograph *Migrant*, the prints of which, now yellowed, I still have.

A huge white auxiliary schooner named *Ramona* that occasionally dropped anchor offshore was owned by a man named Guernsey Curran. It, too, boasted a large crew, some of whom waved to me from the railing when I circled it in the catboat. A year or two later, with the outbreak of World War II, an early warning aircraft identification station was built just off the tee on No. 6. My father was the station's designated air warden, and Curran was one of the volunteers who manned it around the clock. I stood a few four-hour watches with him, the two of us, field glasses to our eyes scanning the skies, very serious and very keen to spot and call into Mitchell Field anything we saw that looked like a possible threat to New York, all the while nattering away like magpies. I can't recall what we talked about, but he seemed to me a benign uncle, and I always looked forward to being on watch with him.

National was truly a unique place, a bastion, really, of a once-was lifestyle. Next to National, for example, atop a steep sand bluff overlooking Peconic Bay, was the huge main house of what then was known as either the Sabin or the Davis estate, take your pick. It had been the summer home of a New York banker named Charles H. Sabin. His widow married Dwight F. Davis, a prominent politician and turn-of-the-century (the "old" turn-of-the-century) tennis notable who among other things was responsible for the Davis Cup. The estate was complete with massive stone gates and a picturesque gatehouse, so picturesque it could have been the inspiration for one of those saccharine "paintings" mass-produced by a California entrepreneur named Thomas Kinkade. In summers the main house was occupied as was the gatehouse, the latter by the chauffeur and his family, which included a boy about my age with whom I occasionally swam and went sailing, clamming, and fishing. Years later the estate was purchased from the Widow Davis by a New York City labor union as a family vacation retreat for its membership. Now it's the site of an upscale Jack Nicklaus–designed private golf club called Sebonack.

Sic transit and all that.

· **19** ·

Never Again

SOME YEARS AGO Greg Norman said he thought technological advances in equipment over the past thirty or so years have rendered many of the world's classic golf courses obsolete, in particular the Old Course at St. Andrews, golf's Holy Land. He might have added to advances in the tools with which the game is played such recent phenomena as "lively" balls that strain the regulatory limits of golf's ruling bodies, plus workout and diet regimens that have turned many of today's top-drawer players into exemplars of physical fitness.

What Norman meant is that because today's superstars can hit the ball such prodigious distances, the Old Course now is too easy and thus no longer viable as a major championship venue (the British Open, for example). Another way of saying the same thing is the often-heard complaint that today's golf courses are "running out of real estate," meaning there simply isn't room to stretch existing holes to challenge the hitting power of a John Daly or a Tiger Woods. When a classic and venerated 466-yard par-5 hole can be reached with a drive and a 7-iron (the famed Road Hole on the Old Course), something essential to the game's well-being has been lost. The counter seems to be to "trick up" designs of new golf courses and renovations of existing courses with excessive bunkering, absurd island greens, barrier plantings—anything to thwart 300-yard-plus drives and 150-yard wedges. Accordingly, bird's-eye views of many of today's championship venues suggest layouts resembling boards on pinball games.

Lost in the scramble to cope with the radical developments that today bear witness to a game in transition is much of golf's original charm. While always a business, it has become big business, and in the interest of ever-rising annual sales curves it has been forced to sacrifice much of its traditional essence, much of its inherent joy. It has become a game with which—to again paraphrase Bobby Jones—my father and his peers would not have been familiar.

It seems to me what has happened is that the game no longer is *played* but rather is worked at. Struggle has replaced fun. The current insane and completely unrealistic emphasis on scoring, on hitting the ball a mile, has leached away much of the pleasure once derived from simply having the leisure to be outside on a benign day, to feel the warmth of the sun, to savor at least reasonably fresh air, to smell newly mown grass, to enjoy the songs and flight of birds, to watch the tumbling, scampering play of squirrels. Despite contentions to the contrary, golf is not a metaphor for life, not a grim struggle to get from one day to the next. It's a game, a game to be enjoyed.

The culprit in all this is television. The very best golfers in the world can be seen on the tube on any weekend year-round. Observing that, physically at least, these paragons of the game appear to be not unlike the rest of us, we find it difficult to accept that we can't do as they do. But we try. Oh, boy, do we try! Lessons and more lessons, the latest equipment gimmick, the new "hot" ball, stroke-saving golf shoes, hours and hours on a practice range . . . the lot of it having little if anything to do with golf, with the pleasures the game affords. Thus we take the sinking of a thirty-foot putt not as the minor miracle it is but as our due for all the work we've put in, for all the money we've spent. If we knock a greenside bunker shot within a foot of the pin, we don't say to ourselves "Wow!" and enjoy the inner glow bringing off such a shot affords. Rather, we say, "That's more like it. That's the kind of shot I'm *really* capable of—not that skulled clunker I hit back on No. 4." When it comes to golf, delusion reigns; we simply can't believe or accept that the skulled clunker from the bunker is the norm, not the exception.

I ventured above the opinion that TV is the culprit, the great corrupter. Yet predating television, the ultimate folly was the asinine linking of golf to machismo. Men, especially young men, tend to bring to the game the need to prove their worth, that they're the equal of the next fellow. They think if Joe Longknocker can smack a drive 280 yards down the middle time after time, "I can, too." No you can't. You *can* build a bookshelf, change your car's oil, whip up a great shrimp gumbo—all abilities that Joe Longknocker does not have—yet you feel his 280-yard drives somehow diminish you in the estimation of the world, and therefore you must equal and perhaps surpass them. The downside of the revolution in club technology is that it's pretty much meaningless in the hands of a duffer; the only ones to really benefit are the very best players.

Exceptions aside, women tend to play this game as it was meant to be played. Some women can be terribly, painfully competitive (or just painful) in a strict golf sense, but most women golfers aren't burdened by delusions, by expectations beyond what they know to be their limitations. They play for the pleasure of playing, for the sociability the game affords, and they play by the rules. They bunt the ball out there however many yards and are delighted when it stays in the fairway. If you want to witness real golfing joy, watch Mom's expression when her tee shot on a par-3 lands and stays on the green. If she two-putts for a par, her day is made. Should she sink a putt for a birdie, she may even spring for the postplay drinks. In contrast, a man would accept the par—the birdie, too—as his due.

Golf is one of the most (if not *the* most) difficult games to play. No two shots are alike, no two results the same. Accordingly, it is pure folly to expect to perform on a par (no pun intended) with the icons of the game, most of whom, these days especially, have been at it since the age of eight or even younger. Yet when it comes to golf, gullibility ranks right up there with breathing. We actually try to absorb the mumbojumbo of golf lessons, the jargon and trappings of which have become as arcane as those of nuclear physics. We buy books and subscribe to magazines that assure us we, too, can reach the Promised Land of even-par; all we need to do is swing like Tiger Woods, which—if we could—would obviate the perceived need to buy the book or subscribe to the magazine.

The Old Man would have been appalled by all this. Oh, don't misunderstand—he would have been busy in the countinghouse along with everyone else dependent upon the game for his or her daily bread. At the same time, however, he would have been aware that something had gone out of it, that somehow golf was diminished. Now it's all in such dead earnest, far removed from the spirit of and psychic income to be derived from grabbing a club and a couple of balls and getting in three or four knockaround holes before dark.

When I was a kid, there was in Yonkers, just north of New York City, a public golf course called Grassy Sprain. No longer existent, it was designed by a man named Devereux Emmet, a member of one of America's leading families and a friend of Charles Blair Macdonald. But despite its patrician breeding, at Grassy Sprain on any day of the week, especially on Saturdays, you'd find Artie from the Sunoco station on Central Avenue locked in mortal combat with Vinny from the Bronx. Artie and Vinny and their counterparts played match play (usually a couple of dollars Nassau and maybe quarter skins), and anything short of a full nelson applied—opportune coughs, sneezes, dropped clubs, dropped bags, cleared throats, movement at the top of backswings, calling out to a third guy in a foursome as the second was about to hit his shot . . . that sort of thing. On the first tee one time, a guy who caned chairs, of all things, had started his downswing when his opponent faced down the fairway and hollered, "Fore!"

Was it golf? Perhaps not, not to a purist, anyway. But it was fun. Those guys played the ball down and couldn't be paid to concede a putt. They *enjoyed* the game, and if there was any postplay griping it was bemoaning the loss of a few bucks, not a rehashing of I couldda, I shouldda, and why-didn't-I.

Another thing about Grassy Sprain is that you played it as you found it. If the fairways were less than lush, the greens perhaps worn and a bit bumpy, the bunkers less than smoothly raked, their perimeters shaggy, so be it; that was the track to be played, period, or as comedian Jimmy Durante might have put it, "Them's the conditions what prevailed." Now, again thanks to television, golfers feel somehow they're getting less than value if the turf off which they play isn't immaculate, if the greens aren't billiard table–smooth, or if the bunker sand isn't consistent throughout.

People watch the Masters on TV, listen to the fawning commentary, and get the impression that's how a golf course should look, not appreciating that labor-intensive Augusta

National has been brought to its absolute peak of condition for that one tournament. It would be a catastrophe if the azaleas didn't bloom on schedule. Obviously the course is in first-rate condition at other times of the year as well, but it, too, is subject to the vagaries of weather, disease, irrigation system ruptures, equipment failures, and every other thing that on a golf course can go awry. It helps, too, that during the hot summer months Augusta National is closed to play.

Golf course superintendents at clubs throughout the nation have to deal with ever-changing greens committees unable to understand why old Siwash Valley doesn't look like the courses its members see on TV. Yet these same greens committees are quick to veto superintendents' requests for additional personnel or for new equipment. Even with additional personnel and the very latest in turf care equipment, expecting a course to always look like the championship venues seen on television is unrealistic. What's more, *it isn't golf*, just as rolling the ball over prior to hitting a shot isn't golf. A less than pristine track is a less than pristine track for everyone who plays it, so as your score soars, railing against ankle-deep roughs or bald spots on fairways is pointless.

The plea here is to *play* the game, to enjoy it as it was meant to be enjoyed, to give up today's unrealistic and seemingly universal obsession with shooting low scores. The question to be asked isn't, "What did you shoot?" but rather, "Did you have a good time?"

The Founding Father, Part II

I THINK ABOUT HIM A LOT, see in myself many of the things I saw in him, and I've come to recognize and understand his essential loneliness. I don't drink as much as he did (he was a Good Time Charlie as opposed to a boozer) and I've had the advantages of a better education, but like Pop I'm sentimental and want to be thought well of by my peers. I also have thin skin and am quick to sense anything less than outright approval. What I don't have is the Old Man's optimism. To him tomorrow was going to be *the* day, the day his ship would come in. He never went out the door headed for a horse-racing park thinking anything other than that was the day he was going to beat the "iron men," as he referred to pari-mutuel betting machines.

I often wonder if he knew his ship indeed had already come in, that it took the form of loving his family and being loved by them in return, of providing well for them, of having the regard and affection of most of those who knew him, and of reaching the top of his profession. For years he carried in his wallet a yellowed newspaper clipping from 1936 reporting that Grantland Rice, then the nation's premier sportswriter, after playing Maidstone's two courses pronounced them "the best conditioned in the country."

There are a lot of things to remember, things I couldn't forget if I tried. Mainly I remember that he cared—cared about his family, about his friends, about this country, about the golf courses of which he was the superintendent. I don't recall either my brother or me ever wanting for anything. We might not get something we wanted right off the bat, but eventually Pop would come through, perhaps not always in the form my brother or I had in mind (for example, I wanted a first baseman's mitt but instead got a catcher's mitt and thereafter was a catcher), but fulfillment nonetheless. My mother was modest in her needs, yet she, too, never wanted for anything except possibly more of his time and attention. Thankfully, she possessed a marvelous and infectious sense of humor I'm sure tided her over the rough spots in her life.

As I recall, only on Sundays, his official day off, did my father not drive over just about every foot of National's roads, stopping to inspect certain greens and tee areas and making notes of pin flags that needed replacing, of a tee bench that needed repair or a fresh coat of paint, of ball washers that needed their towels changed, of tee markers that needed to be repositioned, of outlying areas that needed mowing, brush cut back, roughs dump-raked. He was quick to pick up stray bits of paper, toss aside twigs that had blown down in a high wind, pick up a shovel or rake or some other item of equipment that had fallen off one of the trucks. And of course he always was on hand to supervise the various work-gang projects — top-dressing the greens, resodding the bank of a tee, spraying to ward off or treat a fungal disease, aerating the greens, repairing a bunker washed out by a heavy rain . . . whatever.

Toward the end of his time at National, more often than not he was accompanied on these rounds by the professional, Alick Gerard. The Old Man was generous with his knowledge and passed it along freely to Gerard, considered by my father to be a worthy peer, even a confidant. Thus all the professional's questions were answered in detail, the golf course's care and feeding procedures delineated, the biology, botany, entomology, and chemistry involved explained. Pop held back nothing and in fact was pleased a man he liked took such an interest in a job my father thought was little appreciated.

I have no evidence of this, but I'm convinced that following these rounds with my father Gerard spent evenings making notes of what he had learned. At the end of the 1943 season, when Pop was let go, guess who was appointed National's greenkeeper. Gerard thus became a two-hatter — National's superintendent as well as its professional, the latter post taken over by Alick Gerard Jr. at the start of the 1948 season. (At one time I worked for showman Mike Todd, and he used to say the trouble with the movie business was "too much nephewism." Golf affords no exception.) The senior Gerard continued as National's greenkeeper until 1958, when he retired. Again I have no hard evidence of this, but I can't help but think my father was a victim of the other man's less than up-front intentions.

Keep in mind that golf course superintendents, like magazine editors and managers of Major League baseball teams, are subject to dismissal by whim. A new chairman of a club's greens committee can decide he doesn't like the way the greenkeeper parts his hair, and it's down the road for the greenkeeper. A prolonged period of unusually dry weather can bake a golf course to such an extent its overtaxed irrigation system can't cope. Who's responsible for the resultant off-color and rock-hard greens, the burned-to-a-crisp fairways? Obviously the greenkeeper. A famed one-time Daytona race car owner and crew chief named Smokey Yunick used to say drivers of race cars were like lightbulbs—you screw one out and a replacement in. So it is with golf course superintendents; many let go from one job get another one just down the road or in the next town over. It isn't exactly an itinerant profession but certainly one in which it pays to be adaptable.

In spite of the always present uncertainty inherent in the job, I doubt the Old Man would have preferred a different one. He was good at what he did and was proud of it. When an ailing green was brought back to thriving health, for example, he relished the turnaround, often remarking to my mother that she should see how nicely No. 2, say, had filled in. He really did know his business and, as I've indicated, would impart willingly any pertinent information requested.

He knew his peers, too—not only fellow greenkeepers but many of the metropolitan New York area club professionals, as well, especially the old Scotsmen. An in-car game we'd play when on a family trip would be for him to ask me, as we passed a golf course, to name the professional or the greenkeeper, sometimes both. As a little kid my game favorite was passing a certain course I recall as being just off Long Island's Jericho Turnpike.

"What golf course is that?" the Old Man would ask.

"Wheatley Hills," I'd reply.

"And who's the pro at Wheatley Hills?"

That was my cue to shine. "Willie Klein!" I'd shout, my answer always triggering a smile from him and a hoot of laughter from me.

Occasionally an unknown car would pull into the yard at National, and a man who was a stranger to me would get out and come to the cottage door. Pop would answer the man's knock, then either bid his visitor enter or walk with him back to his car. More often than not these impromptu visitors were his fellow greenkeepers, some seeking his professional advice, some asking if he knew of any job openings, some down on their luck and seeking to put the arm on him (Pop was always good for a ten-spot). One persistent caller (so persistent it got to the point that when he showed up Pop would groan and my mother and I would try to stay out of sight) was an out-of-work greenkeeper who shall, as they say, remain nameless. My father finally managed to steer him to a job in, I believe, New Jersey, the upshot of which was that once the guy was employed the Old Man couldn't get him on the phone.

As mentioned earlier, often knocking on the cottage door were supplicants hoping my father would hire them. These men often brought with them something in the form of a mild bribe, usually a fresh-caught weak fish or bluefish, a striped bass, a pheasant, a dozen fresh eggs, a few dozen clams in a gunny sack, or a plucked, headless, and gutted chicken. When Pop was at Sunningdale the gift bearers' offerings tended to be gallons of homemade red wine, referred to by both the donors and my father as "guinea red," or almost-black Italian cigars tied together in a bunch with a hunk of coarse string and referred to as "guinea stinkers."

An indelible memory of National is my bringing home an old golf club, approximately a mid-iron, made by Tom Morris. Yes, that Tom Morris, the elder Tom Morris. It was given to me by a kid with whom I went to school, a kid named Victor Kromko. He and his mother and father and perhaps a sister lived fairly near the school in a rundown shacklike house. One afternoon I walked home with him, me pushing the bicycle I often rode to and from school. We must have been talking about golf in some way because he volunteered that there was an old golf club in a barrel in a small shed at the side of the family's modest vegetable garden. He asked if I'd like to see it, and unable to think of any reason to say no I said yes. We entered the shed and he started to rummage around in the barrel; in there were upended hoes, a shovel or two, some stakes for tomatoes, odds and ends of old lumber, and the golf club. Its head was rusty, of course, but its shaft was straight, its thick suede grip, although filthy, was intact, and the whipping was unfrayed. I'm sure I admired the club, for my host asked if I'd like to have it. Mindful that I had only a couple of clubs of my own, I said I would, whereupon he said it was mine. I thanked him and pedaled home, anxious to show my father my new club. And when I did, it was the last I saw of it.

(No, I'm wrong. Years later I saw it cleaned up and displayed on a wall in the USGA's Golf House when that fascinating institution, now in Far Hills, New Jersey, was located at 40 East Thirty-eighth Street in Manhattan. Its display card read, "Mid-iron by Old Tom Morris, circa 1875. Gift of William Kilpatrick." Him, not me.)

The last I saw of him was on the lower level of Grand Central Station. He and my mother had come into town on the train from Connecticut to spend a couple of days with me, my wife, and our three children. While the visit was to family, and all that, the really important purpose of the trip was to "battle the iron men" during either Aqueduct's or Belmont Park's fall meeting.

My family and I lived in a large apartment on Manhattan's West Side at Seventy-fifth Street and West End Avenue. Pop's routine during visits was to have a leisurely breakfast, then stroll down to a newsstand on Seventy-second Street and

Broadway at about ten o'clock, buy a *Morning Telegraph* and a *Racing Form*, and take the subway out to the track. He'd study both publications during the trip out to Long Island, and by the time he reached his destination he'd have made a selection to win the first race and would have settled on two or three possibilities to win the second race, giving him what he deemed a good shot at hitting the Daily Double. Once at the track he'd buy a grandstand seat and stop to exchange greetings or to chat here and there with various track personnel with whom he had become acquainted over the years — ushers, pari-mutuel clerks, bartenders, fellow punters.

On such days we'd expect him back at the apartment around 6:00 or 6:30, and when he walked in the door you knew right away what kind of a day he'd had. If the grin was wide, the step lively, the chatter buoyant you knew he'd taken a licking. On the other hand if when you answered the doorbell you found him standing there with a sort of hangdog look, you knew he'd come away a winner. The more baleful his expression the greater the extent of his triumph over the "iron men." But of course he was much too sunny an individual to sustain the pose for long; within a few minutes of his tail-between-his-legs entrance he'd admit somewhat sheepishly that he'd had a pretty good day.

On the occasion during which I saw him for the last time he had come home with the ominous expression but, grinning, soon proposed to take my mother and the five of us out to dinner, admitting he'd had a winning day. We went to a superb Italian restaurant called Capri, then on Fifty-second Street between Broadway and Eighth Avenue, and there in a semiprivate room behind the kitchen had a Lucullan feast topped off with an Italian cheesecake I had never eaten before and haven't been able to find since.

The next morning, their suitcases packed, I went with my parents and my oldest son in a cab to Grand Central. Their train to New Haven was to leave from one of the lower-level tracks. Some two years before he had had a heart attack, and I was worried about him. I tried to carry the luggage, but no, he could handle it, thanks. But as we approached the train he was breathing heavily and obviously laboring. When the four of us embraced and said our good-byes moments before they entered the car of their choice, I couldn't help but feel all was not well. His face was ashen.

Epilogue

POP DIED in Grace-New Haven Hospital a month later. He had come home at the end of the day, had a neat scotch and water chaser while he watched the news on TV, then had his dinner. Soon thereafter he began to experience chest pains. His doctor was called and within a few minutes he was in an ambulance en route to the hospital, my mother at his side and holding his hand. She later said that at one point during the ride in from Branford he looked up at her and said, "Well, kid, I wonder if this is the end of your Old Man?"

My brother, a Branford, Connecticut, attorney, called me to say Pop had had another heart attack and had been taken to the hospital. I told him I was on my way, but my brother said it wasn't necessary, that Pop was resting comfortably and I needn't come up from New York until morning.

The next morning my mother called at about seven o'clock and tearfully reported, "Willie, he's gone." He had suffered a third and massive coronary his once-rugged seventy-four-year-old body simply was unable to withstand.

A day or so later, my brother (himself no longer among those present) told me that a little after midnight on the morning Pop died he had gone up to see him and to say goodnight. He found him sitting on the edge of his bed outside a mandated oxygen tent, his arms and chest wired to various monitoring devices.

"How are you?" my brother asked.

"I'm okay, lad," said Pop, smiling and glancing at one of the oscilloscopes. "I'd really like to break wind, but I'm afraid I'd blow up all these bloody machines."

I can't tell you how much I miss him.

Acknowledgments

NO BOOK PROGRESSING from manuscript to the stalls is a solo effort; along the way a number of people are involved in the process, and this book is no exception.

Accordingly I'd like to thank Rob Taylor, my patient and helpful editor; his equally helpful assistant, Courtney Ochsner; copy editor Sara Springsteen, whose sharp eye and thoughtfulness spared me a number of literary gaffes; John McCreary, who took and gave me the various photos of the National Golf Links of America; Mel Lucas, past president of the Golf Course Superintendents Association of America (GCSAA), who provided valuable information about now-historic golf course maintenance equipment; Marvin E. Newman, who took the stunning aerial photo of National's fourteenth hole; Peter Cookingham of Michigan State University, who pointed me in the direction of certain source material;

Randall Herring, National's former manager and a boyhood friend; Debbie Smith of mower manufacturer Jacobsen, a Textron Company; and Lindsay S. Totino, curator of collections at the New York Yacht Club.

Finally, I'd like to tip my hat to the nifty lady with whom I share the premises, my dear wife, Phyllis, who believed and encouraged.